EXPLORING YOUR HUMANITY

Exploring Your Humanity

Journey to Awakened Consciousness

By

Paula A Bourassa

Copyright © 2023 Paula A Bourassa

All rights reserved.

First Printing: 2023
ISBN: 978-0-9993197-6-5
ISBN: 978-0-9993197-9-6 (e)
Library of Congress Control Number: 2023902909
Appleton, Wisconsin

Dedicated
To anyone who is choosing to wake up.

Table of Contents

Forward ix
Awakening 1
Married to Self 4
Humans Being Anonymous 9
Burnout and Wanting to Die 19
You Are What You Believe & Create Accordingly 32
Self-Respect vs. Masked Consciousness Demands 62
Funeral for a Friend 69
A New Self Emerged 71
Channeled Messages on Awakening 75
Epilogue - Ascension Note 97

Forward

One day driving along, I looked up at the blue sky and experienced clear tuition of this being my last human incarnation. Even though I cannot support this experience with concrete evidence, it was one thing that did not require proof. You just know. A knowing that defies explanation or reason and chimes with a confirmation you accept without reservation or need to challenge on any level. The deep resonance is symbolic of living in an awakened reality, where you lean on the outpourings of your inner world rather than adopting what is broadcast on social media, tv programming, or the news.

A significant challenge of being awake may be that you won't be able to provide satisfactory answers for those who choose to remain in deep slumber. They will question your ways, so it will be paramount to remember that their code of ethics comes from the brainwashing of governing societal rules on politics, religion, medicine, and/or any organized platform promoting practices on how you should live. Reason enough to examine every belief to ascertain if it matches your sacred inner knowing. Find any deterrent to your God-given right to be happy, joyous, and free.

I'd been dealt hand after hand of opposition from those closest to me and in every possible relationship where I have loved someone and hoped to be loved in return, yet opposition poured in from every direction. The heartache, pain, and suffering rendered me near dead. Without awareness, I would have died a slow death of depression, rotting my insides, becoming sickened from it all, and quietly passing away. I chose to remain instead. I initially thought I must have incurred some lousy karma or be a slow learner to endure such punishment, rejection, and abandonment in a single lifetime, but come to find out, that is what it took for me to break free and be something other than a victim of circumstance.

We all have great beauty, strength, and the potential for great ugliness and weakness. The key is knowing the difference and when to embrace thought forms that instigate doubt, fear, greed, or hostility, before they can act out. In terms of feeling personally hurt, it would be easy to see how someone else might derive perceptions about life differently from mine because how could you expect anyone to understand what it feels like to have walked in your shoes. Only you can be genuinely congruent within. You cannot leave your well-being up to anyone else, no matter how much they love you, because their ability to show love and care will be based on their own ability to love and care for themselves, nothing else.

Spiritual growth is not about changing others and the world but an inside job of changing yourself. In this timing of Ascension, it came on full, as the dark was exposed to the light. Not wanting to miss out on my chance to ascend, I claimed my sovereign rights as a child of God and am present to share my journey.

Awakening

There was no specific event that activated my awakening process. It was more like a series of ongoing aftershocks, with each successive jolt triggering an emotional shake-up of old belief systems. The process would leave me feeling shaken, as everything I had thought to be true was shown to be fraught with contradiction. Before that point, I examined what I believed to understand how those beliefs came to be and why. I was choosing to accept the new wave of spiritual growth, so investigating new perspectives and ideas ensued to clear my pounding head.

As layer upon layer of societal consciousness unwound, I would eventually adjust to the unraveling and continue expanding my awareness. Still, I constantly scanned for each go-round start and finish point. After dealing with so many turbulent processes, I wanted to guesstimate a finish point to avoid further anxiety and have some relief. It was more accurate to say the expansion is ongoing, which eases the journey by eradicating any judgment for not arriving at the finish line sooner.

Life is goal-driven to the point that if you spend most of your time advancing toward a start and finish marker, you could miss unexpected assistance via forces of energy existing outside those boundaries. It would be difficult to label or define the experience except to say the pathway has included many undefined off-track developmental phases. Without conscious awareness and the magic of your intuition in conjunction with Universal assistance, these guideposts could go unclaimed if you stay on a fast track driven only to execute a timely finish. Best to remove those blinders and open your field of vision.

Journey to Awakened Consciousness

What you resist does persist. I felt many times that I'd drifted wayward. However, looking back on my foibles, it seems most remarkable I would draw to myself the very thing I'd spent a lifetime trying to avoid. After concentrated efforts to veer attention away from a person, place, or thing, the momentum would accumulate, revealing smack dab in front of my face a manifestation of what I feared or detested most. Then the most notable observation... watching other people become or develop a tendency into the things they despised too.

This universal law is not meant to cause you misery, but instead, presents an opportunity to help shift your perspective and open your conscious awareness enough to realign this human being phenomena. For instance, when you are traveling through an old neighborhood filled with memories and have the momentary thought or dread of running into someone specific from your past and, BAM, there is the person right in front of you. Once you garner the lesson, you'll experience true freedom and be able to go anywhere and feel prepared, no matter who you might encounter.

Since you can spend an entire lifetime trying to figure things out, relaxing by allowing yourself to make changeovers naturally, like the four seasons, is better. It is exhausting trying to get things right when, in truth, you will find a balance point by remembering it most likely took just as many times to get it wrong. Believe it or not, being and breathing will get you there!

Do you believe everything you hear or rely on your inner instrument if something doesn't feel credible? An example would be when you have nagging inklings something is wrong and barge past it anyway. Nothing worse than the massive regret that sweeps overhead because you didn't listen to that gut feeling in the first place.

There is great strength and power in realizing how often you may have yelled over your intuition, simply bowled over it with blasting

Exploring Your Humanity

mental gyrations. It may not sound like much, but once you are willing to hear and feel your inner voice, you can trust its soft, vulnerable whisper to nurture a loving union within yourself. When I don't minimize myself, there is less chance of taking something important to you for granted, so any other mutual partnership will also be a marriage based on every voice having merit. A marriage to self is based on a loving union within each person first and then the amalgamation of a loving partnership with anyone or anything else. This automatically includes honoring and respecting Earth.

Married to Self

It's enough to be and express who I am without the measure of victory being threaded to another person's version of opulence.

Every turn you make in 3D wants to dictate your worth or exposes you to a trend-of-the-day smear campaign on what you need to do to have value. It takes guts to honor, care for, and love yourself. But once you claim this union with yourself, you've got it all in this lifetime.

The challenge is that we all have a distinctly human need to be loved and approved of, to feel a part of, and not alone. That is why the task of achieving total self-care can feel daunting because, many times, there will be no one in sight to give you a hug or congratulate you on the progress you've made. No one to cheer you on. No one, or not many before you, has made this claim to the degree of claiming sovereign rights, so it's not like you can search the web for a video on how to do it; you become the role model, you're it!

You pioneer your way, and the glory is that once you've reached the goal and all parts of your inner self are merged, nothing can touch that. The satisfaction is knowing you can handle anything the external world may throw at you. It can feel like you are fighting with a vast army of warriors all by yourself, and though they are only aspects (lifetime traits past, present, future), you know you've fought the good fight. You need not belabor the matter because you realize by making allowances for *your little personality warriors*, you've created a peace treaty rather than banishing them to another war of self-criticism.

The ways and means you've dealt with every part of yourself are of tremendous value to mass consciousness because if one day,

Exploring Your Humanity

another person chooses to look at their warrior, they've got a battleplan to perceive, someone else's strategy, which in reviewing may activate their creative forces on waging a 'good fight.' Yes, it is an invisible forcefield of energy, but still, one never knows when another human being may feel the impetus or be ready to face themselves. At this time, these thought forms and ideas are available for support in the cosmos.

As you ponder, wonder, or think about how to help yourself, you are like a magnet and will draw this support from those who've travailed the pathway before you. Thoughts are living things, so ideas on how they were able to sort themselves out are there for you to pull down. It is a gloomy task at times, but the reflection of light at the end of the tunnel gives enough hope to prevail.

If you've ever sat and cried your eyes out, you know firsthand about longing and yearning for comfort, yet the real pain comes from believing comfort is outside you someplace. *The job is complete when you see what you've been craving is the comfort you can give yourself.* Self is the only qualified agent for the job because no one else has walked your pathway, so they couldn't possibly know what it feels like, where it comes from, or what it means. The marriage of self is sacred because the union is a powerful reflection for everyone. Because one has contacted and unified with 'the self,' it is naturally possible for others to do the same. In short, like being available in the air that you breathe.

Nature gives us many examples of supreme linking too. Sea turtles know the minute they hatch to head for the sea, and the salmon silently directed each year to swim back to their origins are a few demonstrations of connectedness miracles. In a literal sense, for example, one country is the first to land on the moon. Well, before long other countries are inspired and motivated to achieve the same. Same here, only with the personal process; it doesn't need to be broadcast via media outlets. It simply goes out into the ether and becomes available to the rest of mankind because all subconscious minds are connected.

You seek answers to some of life's tough questions while on Earth; however, until you ascend or transition, those answers have previously felt hidden. As awakened beings, they become accessible, so you need not perish just to reach that level of understanding. In this timing of Ascension, you become the other side, as all sides blend into one and any realm that has dwelt closely to Earth from the beginning. The Ascended Earth will be a collection of many layers of strata, so no surprise, if you start to see and feel that merger within your unique sensitivity. An example of my experience is becoming aware that long-term grief has lessened greatly because it seems the veil separating the other realms is nearly non-existent.

You are awakening when you know it is time to heal the unbearable grief of those outside fixes not curing you. In the meantime, it's your job to disband the pain of thinking it's someone else's job to take care of you or feel everyone else needs to understand where you're coming from to feel okay with them and the rest of the world. When others appear unreachable and unavailable for communication, with a heightened sense of aloneness, embrace the lockdown with self. Well worth going through some restlessness for the cause, and if you can avoid falling into that age-old pit of finding a distraction, you are sure to stay on track, making remarkable speed toward your goal.

Maybe times past, you could fill up with food, drink, shopping, sex, or gambling, but it somehow stopped soothing, so recall that feeling and stick with the lockdown. We've all stepped in at one time or the other. I made it a point to forgive myself when I put on a few extra pounds before knowing what was happening. A part of me knew I was comfort eating but could not stop. I was craving the comfort of anything, so moving forward, I couldn't put myself in a sling over it either because I had experienced enough harsh

Exploring Your Humanity

treatment from myself. Maybe you can recognize sooner that if you're attempting to comfort yourself with an old fix but know you are ready to heal, take the band-aid off and be gentle. Heal by your divine self-care and attention.

We need more than a few brave ones who will soldier the consequences of bucking the system to gain freedom…as much as you can in this mechanical and robot-like world. Someone who will reflect what is needed for each person to live on a lighted Earth. Someone who, no matter what can manage a few words of kindness even when they feel rebuked, provoked, or castigated.

Some of what I have disclosed in this writing is to ignite your remembrance of the reasons for folding up and, at the same time, to encourage your unraveling for becoming an awakened being. We can only awaken to ourselves and then hold that light and hope for all to awaken. I didn't know when I looked up to the sky that day with a flash of this being my last walk on Earth that it would include striving to know and honor all aspects of myself. I had no idea then that the purpose of being married to self would be my life's primary mission or that achieving unity within would be an enormous achievement not just for me but automatically gifting to everyone else.

Understanding yourself and how you operate is like a tremendous voluminous novel in which no one can take from you or change the script unless you allow it. The sense of freedom and peace it renders cannot be bought or borrowed. The following chapters help uncover things about yourself that may not have been noticed previously but will undoubtedly be vital if you choose to awaken. Hopefully, you will find a tidbit that inspires your wings of freedom to open as you select a plan of action to understand your internal blueprint.

We all become a part of the platform on which the New Earth will arise like a phoenix bird out of ash. Self-love and acceptance will permeate until every living thing is honored and respected because each human being has gone thru the process, yielding a natural

Journey to Awakened Consciousness

interest in the same happiness and sense of peace for all. Never exploiting anyone or anything to your advantage is a sign that you are awakened. Those who don't choose to awaken will still have an opportunity to continue in the old ways on another planet similar in quality to Earth.

Humans Being Anonymous
Awaken Anonymity

My primary guide showed me that just before coming to Earth, we decide who our parents, family, and friends will be and what agreements we will commit to with those on earth stage with us. Envision a game called Pick a Parent. Behind Door number 1 are Mr. Unemployed and Mrs. Alcoholic Drinker. Behind Door number 2 are Mr. Wife/Child beater and Mrs. Denial. And behind Door number 3 are Mr. College Professor and Mrs. Social Worker. Imagine what parents would best help with the specific lessons you've chosen to learn and who would be most supportive in helping you honor the agreements you made for your lifetime. And since like does attract like, the search includes the best matches (future parent) or soul qualities that are a similar vibration to your own, Notice I mentioned soul qualities, not personality likenesses.

If we understand that we pick and create our experiences on Earth that will best help us remember our divinity, we can drop the role of being a victim and recognize each person's life is part of what they selected to achieve this purpose. The planned journey includes everything you need. All the places you usually feel inclined to visit often will be areas that hold memories from past embodiments. To revisit them is a way to activate the memory that your soul lives on eternally and give balance to any illogical reactivity causing discord in your present now.

For instance, one person may not understand why they fear heights and cannot uncover answers on their present timeline, so they turn to hypnosis or past life regression to solve the mystery. Each incarnation is the personality striving to merge with

Journey to Awakened Consciousness

the soul in [1]At-One-Ment.* Returning to that place of the highest in the ethereal realms is very similar to the place where Mother-Father God resides in each of us.

The solar plexus (located near the naval on our earthly bodies) is the point on the body where the soul resides and the place where you connect with your knowing or gut instinct. It helps us recall that even as alone as we feel, we are never separate from anyone or anything. The soul contains a memory of all that is—being limited to the knowledge that pertains only to the personality expressing itself in the body you currently inhabit in this lifetime mainly occurs because your mind isn't equipped to carry all that information. It stays hidden. If somebody answered how to get out of a maze before you started, there would be no reason to enter.

When you remember we are all soul brothers and sisters with no need to label ourselves or others based on what we do or don't do or what we look like, the concept of infinity is illuminated.

We were whole, to begin with, and then strayed from the ideation of being one with God through free will choices. If it takes a particular soul 3 or 50 lifetimes of drinking and drugging in excess before they bring that aspect of themselves into balance, then so be it. Using m ind-altering substances has always allowed people to experience a different level of consciousness. Many of us have danced to that tune at one time or another, but if used excessively, we may finally be complete with missing out on life's

---

[1] *As freewill beings and co-creators with God, we had minds with which to build, but we created thought forms and desire patterns that deviated from the Law of One. Over time these separate projections imprisoned our consciousness. Finally, we came to a point where we were lost; we lost awareness of our oneness with God and our ability to move back to Him in consciousness. The Edgar Cayce Primer'*

Exploring Your Humanity

important moments. Navigating from a sober perspective allows for heightened awareness and receiving guideposts that point to the highest good and joy. In the grand circle of anonymity, we can either continue using drugs and alcohol or stop the dance of addiction to heal. Once unburdened, we send out a telepathic signal for others to receive the thought form as an option. It is a beautiful way to free your soul, get closer to knowing your God-self, and uplift the energy of addiction on the entire planet. It's all for the one and one for all in this unlimited universe, so there is never only one reason for doing anything.

If it takes a soul an entire lifetime of running away from relationships, no one can say nothing was garnered from all that running. It is interesting what we call success or failure. If a person is happily married for fifty years, we say it was a success. If someone is divorced three to four times or leaves this earthly life, never having been married, we say, "Oh, poor so and so."

We call someone in jail a terrible person and someone who does charity work a wonderful person. It's one thing to commit a crime against another human being, but many times as deeply felt to perpetuate a crime against self. In the end, God loves us whether we can honor all our agreements or not. That is reflected in the ability to reincarnate, or in simple terms, get another chance to try again.

I have known people who continue to make the same choices repeatedly. Someone could steal, gamble, or break the law continually, end up in prison each time, or keep do-gooding for others until they drop dead from exhaustion from lack of self-care. It is not for us to weigh such a thing to decide which is worse. We judge others and ourselves because it leaves us with confidence and superiority, as if we know the better way to proceed, but that is for God to evaluate.

Journey to Awakened Consciousness

Everybody feels their way to be the right way, which leaves little space or allowance for anyone else's way. Hence, the leading loss of life in our world and the religiously instigated notion implying, "My God is better than your God." This school of thought has taken us to war for centuries. One of the most profound things I have ever seen is a plaque on an entrance wall at the Museum of Diaspora in Israel that states, "How could one loving God not honor all forms of worship." Believing you have the right way is how you protect yourself from vulnerability and stay in the safety of a dominating mind-ruling mode suggesting that you have all the answers. Sadly, this only takes you on a detour from your heart center.

See how you feel if you allow yourself the awareness that all the ways you have known and believed to be true may not be. Many people gravitate toward mainstream thought to feel self-assured rather than take the time to identify how they are feeling about their own beliefs.

The impending uneasiness left me wobbly when spiritual awareness opened more unlimited thinking and made me start questioning what I thought I knew versus the knowledge I had just acquired. Being insistent that my way was the only way helped me feel safe, as it is for anyone who is adamant about an issue yet unwilling to hear another viewpoint.

When you learn that a child has been born, send out a thought of love and support for all that being has chosen and agreed to do on their earthly sojourn. Let that acceptance and open-mindedness be your shower gift. We all come here to heal ourselves and those we connect with during our current lifetime. This purpose is programmed in our psychic anatomy, along with the various agreements we make that will ultimately expand or constrict our souls. What we each agree to may be entirely different, yet what remains the same is the goal of blossoming into the fullness of love that is the fundamental nature of our creation. The

Exploring Your Humanity

softening is that Mother- Father- God loves us the same, expanded or constricted.

We have the technology to check the physical condition of a newborn, yet the vulnerabilities that comprise the whole being and its various lifetimes remain inaccessible. It was meant to be this way. For example, if somebody knew in advance that the newborn would be prone to a violent temper and aggressive behavior as an adult, it would almost certainly interfere with the interaction of all those meant to be involved. If an individual knew in advance the other person's weaknesses and veered away, it would deprive those participants of the soul growth that comes from exploring ways of responding to life lessons.

You might think; If I agreed to that, why don't I remember? What happens is we lose the memory of our agreements so that we can honor them. Many of us say if we remembered, we would never have agreed to some of these experiences before taking on a mortal body. Then, once encumbered in the flesh, it seems almost impossible to understand how we thought we could endure some of these harsh trials.

We forget so much that some of us will even act highly insulted if reminded that nothing that is not agreed upon here happens here. Not one thing. Not one exception. You can tell when someone has forgotten this sacred rule of life about all living things. The number one sign of total amnesia is to hear someone classify themselves or others as helpless victims of circumstance.

Personality may enjoy the benefits of robust ill health; however, the soul knows it is a minor feature compared to the whole or higher self. There are no victims. There are only masters who utilize the power of creation in unique ways. If you had already attained mastery in a past lifetime and ascended, you would not need to return to Earth unless by pure choice. In that instance, you would fully remember who you are and why you've come, as in the

Journey to Awakened Consciousness

case of Ascended Master Saint Germain. Numerous volumes giving varying accounts of the last time he walked here describe that after ascending, he did choose to return to the region of France to unify all of Europe. He was known as the Wonder Man for many reasons, but primarily for his ability to remain present for over 200 years in human form. Only a master would be able to achieve such a feat.

Someone can tap into a person's Akasha (the recorded history of all they have been and done throughout time), but they must be a master themselves. Most importantly, this means you possess no tendency to infringe upon another soul's free will because, as an ascended master, you have already balanced any part of yourself that would tend to falsify or misappropriate energy. You would have graduated from Earth's classroom and learned your lessons, becoming God-like without needing to be recycled back here again.

Each time we return to this plane for another experience, we are assigned guides, guardians, angels, and ascended masters to assist us. Many of these beings have walked here, so they are fully equipped to understand and help us. They will not pull us by the arm over rough terrain but will be happy to offer guidance by suggesting possible ways to get through it. Life's experiences vary for each human being, yet they all weave a similar thread.

I use the term mother below because it is my frame of reference. However, this word includes anyone of any gender who has ever mothered another human being or cared for someone important to them in that way.

There will be the mother who agrees to raise a child with special needs, such as a person with paraplegia or Downs Syndrome. There will be a mother who knows in advance that her child will pass from a cancerous condition at a young age and has chosen (before incarnating back here) the experience as a possible way to expand her ideas and beliefs about life and death. There will be a mother who gives birth to a child and feels depressed immediately afterward,

Exploring Your Humanity

suffering as she realizes she doesn't feel instant love for the child. Talking to a physician about hormones does little to alleviate guilt, yet, knowing it could be a past life memory offers a soothing alternative if it applies.

There will be a mother who signs up for a lifetime with a child who suffers from long-term drinking and drug addiction. There will be a mother whose biggest upset is that her children don't pick up after themselves, drop crumbs on the floor, and leave the lights on. A mother will beat a child and end up on the evening news. There will be a mother who cannot handle the pressure of her family and runs away from home. There will be a mother who cannot tolerate views other than her own and may disown her child for not living a life that complies with her beliefs.

There will be a mother who puts a child up for adoption because her own life is out of control and unmanageable. A mother will give birth and abandon a child in a desolate back alley. There will be a mother who has the perfect experience in all ways. There will be a mother who never has a life of her own but lives her whole life for her child. There will be a mother who agrees to foster a child that needs a home and then suffers from the insecurity of not being the biological parent.

Lastly, a potential mother will find out she cannot bear children but doesn't choose to adopt or foster them either. She will suffer from a lack of worth since our whole world places great value on the female reproductive tract and being able to reproduce. She will feel useless, but so will the mother who feels distraught about raising her biological children, who remain unmanageable, leaving her feeling like a failure. It does get you thinking about which of these scenarios is better or worse. Why is any of them different from the other [2*] if I know I am all of them? Maybe not literally, but certainly because spiritually, I relate and connect to every other being.

Journey to Awakened Consciousness

We all participate in earthly experiences, ultimately leaving us with similar conditions the next time if we cannot learn from our choices. What a hellish drama for the person who never understands but continues the same old thought patterns and reactions, creating abuse for themselves and everyone else. It's bad enough that you may feel judged by others. However, the most profound suffering comes from repeating these old ways of being and how we victimize ourselves.

Over lifetimes, we add up the total of our experiences. You must wonder if it makes a difference whether you've agreed to give up your life at the hand of another or whether you commit the crime by becoming a martyr, extinguishing your own life force. None of these honors the sacredness of the soul in any case.

There are no secrets in this life because there is nothing that you have thought, said, or done that billions of humans have not considered before you. The universe sees all, and the God Force is our supreme authority. It is much easier to leave the evaluating of

---

2 *"When in every condition he receives each event, whether favorable or unfavorable, with an equal mind which neither likes nor dislikes, his wisdom is established, and, having met good or evil, neither rejoiceth at the one nor is cast down by the other. He is confirmed in spiritual knowledge, when, like the tortoise, he can draw in all his senses and restrain them from their wonted purposes."*

The illuminated sage regards with equal mind an illuminated, selfless Brahmin, a cow, an elephant, a dog, and even an outcast who eats the flesh of dogs. Those who thus preserve an equal mind gain heaven even in this life, for the Supreme is free from sin and equal-minded; therefore, they rest in the Supreme Spirit. The Bhagavad Gita'

Exploring Your Humanity

another life to that Supreme Being rather than taking it upon yourselves to determine how someone else should manage to live.

Judging is also a form of resistance to other ways of being and draws the judgmental experiences we detest to us like a magnet. It keeps in play the universal law; *what you resist persists!* This scientific law of *attracting like* is always in operation. It is in fighting and not claiming an aspect of yourself that projects the feature outward, thereby drawing the force of it right back unto yourself.

This mirror effect can assist us in seeing parts of ourselves we may not have formerly brought to consciousness. Once aware of a flawed characteristic, we can get to know it, understand why it exists, and blend it with all our other facets with love. This invisible action renders us less likely to be judgmental, with a greater understanding that we are not separate from anyone else.

Each parent on the face of this Earth will have unique struggles regarding their children's actions, feelings, attitudes, and lifestyle choices. The more they resist, the more these very traits will persist. These struggles are the irritations and aggravations that can push a human being to the limit. They either emotionally explode or find a way that is not destructive to themselves or anyone else. Embracing a philosophy that allows you to live and let live not only brings peace but also holds neutral space for others to feel the consequences of their own decisions rather than insisting on results using forceful tactics.

Then, they can decide whether their choices serve them instead of just rebelling. Once you stop putting restrictive demands on their energy field, they are less inclined to persist. They feel that you are honoring their way of being, and they acknowledge it by taking off the boxing gloves. If the suffering and agony of parenting assist us in this soul process, then there is no need to feel like a failure in any respect.

Journey to Awakened Consciousness

Knowing that the total of our experiences helps us find personal freedom and, ultimately, the way back to Source allows us to view emotional pain as a natural trigger for activating the process. Showing that our troubles are not so much caused by others, but come from inaccurate beliefs we carry about ourselves, is how we identify the root of any internal disturbance and use the opportunity to expand our way of thinking to attain self-mastery.

Making the conscious choice to know your soul is where the Awakening/Ascension Process begins. Before ascension energies rose, the old paradigm consciousness supplied an essential vehicle for growth, learning, and opportunities in this earthly experience because once born, you are a free soul for only a moment. Once you are named and become a labeled entity, you become somebody's something.

You are the property of some family, group, or country. You are each given an identifying number. As a member of a particular clan, you're expected to follow certain family traditions and follow suit, implying that adopting a set of matching beliefs such as *we are lawyers, and that is what you will do as well,* or *we attend Catholic church and so will you* are in order.

When a soul exits or enters, we remark again that this is or was the son or daughter of so and so (or mother, father, aunt, uncle, grandparent, cousin, etc.). Yet, there is that sacred moment between states of human life and the unseen realms of awareness where we remain unclassified. This zone is a place of neutrality with no division but the merger of becoming a brother-sister of everyone else on the planet. Everyone is still family as the soul prepares to reenter the earth plane. There is no thought to compete over money or property because everyone is entitled to the same inheritance—an anonymous state of being where there is no name other than Child of God.

Burnout and Wanting to Die

"And may you find a quiet bench to sit upon in the rose garden, and may you hear and feel the resonance of birds song upon your own breast that is encoded with remembrance for your heart and a memory from whence you've come to soothe your tired soul." (Author unknown)

This writing would not be complete without discussing not wanting to be here. I recall being a teenager and mentioning to someone that I felt like killing myself but didn't feel much better after hearing the person's reply, which indicated that you are not a good person if you feel like taking your own life. I felt ashamed and filled with even more despair, yet it is one of the reasons I set out on a life-long search for more answers than my religious upbringing had provided.

I was thirsty for spiritual knowledge and started by checking to see what other religions taught about life and death. I had been taught about the end of the world and that one day the whole planet would just go kaboom, and life as we know it would be over. This idea had not given me a lot of hope. As a little girl, I would lay awake at night pondering these matters and feeling sure there must be more to the story. It just didn't feel possible that you're dead, buried, and gone forever when you die.

In addition, after losing my best friend in the eighth grade, I was pushed even deeper into myself as I grasped for answers about dying. I reasoned that if my beloved friend was gone for good and life was this short, cut, and dry, I didn't feel like I wanted to be here either. Time does indeed heal everything, but even so, I would never be the same person after her passing. It was a dramatic shift in my

Journey to Awakened Consciousness

early life, and I knew there would be no rest until I had knowledge that would relieve the grief that sickened me and haunted my heart. This started a lifelong quest for information about existing and how it pertains to the true nature of a person's soul. I now know one of these answers involved life being eternal.

I had felt desolation many times since my teenage years, like a human failure, that my life wasn't worth living, so I no longer wanted to be here. My pursuit of life-changing answers provided perks, such as encountering many other like-minded individuals investigating matters of the spirit. Over the years, I've talked to many people who have expressed or experienced the same burnout. Sometimes, all you need to hear is that someone else felt the same way at one time or the other and survived. Anyone who ever confided in me a similar experience felt better for just having the opportunity to speak their truth without being made to feel they were wrong or immoral. Holding the space for people to express themselves without interjecting an opinion is one of the greatest gifts to offer another human being.

We pick our parents and many life experiences, get in the middle, and go, yuck! Even those already awakened start complaining about why life has become dreary and feel they don't have the stamina to continue. Aware or not, you want to die just to be free from it all. Thankfully, even though I've arrived at that point many times, I never went through with it and can be here to share. My belief in reincarnation urged me to stay since I knew if I took my own life, I would return here sooner or later to try again. Extinguishing your life is like putting yourself in jail once you realize the things you hoped to escape are still there and that living out your designated time wasn't such a bad idea.

Through my work as a mental medium, this concept was reinforced, finding that some who crossed over by suicide are more upset once they realize that life does go on, just in a different form,

Exploring Your Humanity

and learning continues on the other side. Since the original thought behind this act is to extinguish that which cannot be extinguished, it leaves many souls who have tried to accomplish this feat feeling confused since there is suddenly the awareness that you still exist, making it difficult at times for them to move onward and embrace their newfound existence in the other dimensions. The essence of reincarnation is the belief in an eternal, indestructible soul in a temporary body, where a spirit seeks wisdom within the confines of that earthly vessel. In each body, the spirit begins with a goal to learn something new on the way to greater wisdom or, eventually, a stage of enlightenment that no longer requires reincarnation. [3*]

There is no need to return to Earth when your body, mind, and spirit unify personality-driven aspects and merge with your higher self. There is no further need to reincarnate once you ascend unless you take a body for other reasons. The step of ascension is your pure, light body returning home into the heart of Mother-Father-God. One of the most well-known who exemplified this ascension progression was Jesus. [4*]

---

[3] *Author's Note: Numerous great thinkers have believed in the soul's migration. The great philosophers Pythagoras, Socrates, Plato, Aristotle, and even Saint Augustine believed in the soul's rebirth. General Patton, Gandhi, Henry Ford, and the Dalai Lama all discussed memories of, or beliefs in, having past lives.*

[4] *Key 315: 132-145 140 This was demonstrated by Jesus when he balanced the basic thirty-two chemical elements in his human body with the thirty-third transformation of Light known as the Lak Boymer.* (This showed how his cellular chemical functions could be completely rebuilt into a Christ body of Light over a three-and-a-half-day cycle, compared to seven years to replace the body cells.) 143 Jesus came to reactivate the chemical blueprint of Light in Man and allow*

Journey to Awakened Consciousness

We are closest to the spirit realm we just left when we first entered the world. As we grow and develop our personalities, somewhat influenced by the belief systems of those nearest us, we are drawn into an ego-based society, forgetting who we are and where we came from. Babies and young children still fresh from the unseen realms seem to see things that are not there, have imaginary playmates, and smile at something unseen. No one has yet administered that first dose of brainwashing, telling them it is impossible to see, hear, or feel spirit. They can envision their angels, fairies playing in the field, or busy little leprechauns running up and down the hallway. No one at this stage of the child's development feels prompted to say that seeing spirit is insane or evil.

Anything people don't understand spiritually, or fear, could make them react by saying it's the work of the Devil. From my understanding, an angel went against God's will and became one called Satan. According to my sources, that prince of darkness also has his light side and has risen to become one with the God Force again. So fallen or ascended, it's all a point of view, depending on whom you're talking to. The old expression, "The devil made me do it," is a classic copout designed to divert blame, and although

---

him to use this as an enabling function for a higher ultrastructure of Light which is the Holy Spirit resonance of the Eternal Light.

*Lak Boymer/Lag Ba'omer According to Enoch, the reprogramming of the human chemistry through the "Divine Wisdom" so that the thirty-two basic chemical building blocks in the human body are coupled with a thirty-third element which is the synthesis of the best attribute and best function of the previous thirty-two elements. The thirty-third element is the implanting of "Divine Wisdom" which alters the vibrations of the physical body and prepares it for reincorporation back into the "Divine Body." "The Keys of Enoch®"

Exploring Your Humanity

humorous to some degree, represents the unaware state of consciousness that still blankets the Earth.

The next time someone speaks to you of the Devil, remind them there is a bit of the Devil in each of us, which explains why seemingly good people do bad things. It doesn't mean they are bad people. It just means that an aspect of them still needs to be brought into balance. No matter a person's station in life, no one exemplifies perfection. We can either act out a devilish aspect of ourselves or simply embrace it. When understood, the temptation factor is no longer in control, and the urge subsides.

For instance, if you recognize the need to steal comes from a part of you that fears you'll never have enough or just wishes to get a one- up on society, you can ask for guidance on tuning into yourself to understand why. Self-knowledge is the missing puzzle piece in solving the issue, and when the need *to take* surfaces, you'll have enough trust in yourself to eventually cease the motion.

The compelling nature of the original thought no longer feels like it has power over you because it has found its duality on the flip side. The union of the two polarities creates oneness and wholeness, leaving no dangling energies to persuade or provoke the individual to act out.

The Devil is an essential ingredient in any religion that preaches redemption. However, in self-discovery mode, you'll find that to overcome evil, one must recognize where it dwells. People must be aware of evil tendencies that reside within them so they don't inadvertently sin against anyone else. Lucifer played out his role in history just like the rest of us. Someone had to be an example of what happens when you make poor choices. Interfering with another person's free will does get you someplace, but it's not glistening in paradise. If you want people to do it your way, you need a pitchfork, and horns would come in handy to fend off any rebels.

Journey to Awakened Consciousness

By the time you reach middle school, you are aware of differences between you and your friends based on what their parent's belief systems taught them. As you go into adolescence, many questions are present. The day's topic is boys and girls and who gets asked out by whom. This is where the pain begins. It includes the doubting and the questions about anything and everything, the major one being why someone is more attractive or well-liked than you are.

As time goes on, the plot thickens. Each person's drama finds a stage, the curtain goes up, and the play continues. As you go into adult life, it intensifies once you realize you are on your own and responsible for taking care of yourself. The intensity grows when your relationships deepen and the need for human bonding increases. Now, you are not only dealing with your desire for happiness but also have the other person's feelings to consider and whether their needs and desires are being met.

God understood it wouldn't be easy and gave us a dispensation by creating much less complicated companions to be with, like cats, dogs, horses, and birds. Even so, there are many ways to love, and an intimate relationship doesn't have to be sexual because it could include anyone you cherish in your life. Pets simply give us a reprieve from the demands of a human union.

Once grown, if you have chosen the experience of having children, you suddenly face another one of life's challenges. You realize that your offspring's choices may be completely different from your own, and if their actions create embarrassing societal problems, you could be prone to take it personally and wonder where you went wrong. Life can become quite overwhelming if you believe that the same rules should apply to all or that you are responsible for another person's actions. It eases parental pressure when you understand that your child chose you, and in turn, you chose your child as part of a soul agreement so everyone would have

Exploring Your Humanity

a chance to grow, learn, and expand simultaneously. This unique being is not your clone just because you gave birth to the person.

Facing your ego can be very challenging. Getting anyone to honor your value system is exhausting, especially when they are unwilling to comply. When you are so fed up with trying to change another person, and they refuse to be swayed, further fatigue sets in as you realize all your efforts were in vain. When you understand that they will not accede to your wishes, you may quickly find a way to remove yourself from their presence and stop all communication. This happens if your objective is egocentric because you lose interest once you can no longer control the pieces on the board.

Unfortunately, the previous is another illusion humans adopt and, in likeness, to the freedom they think they'll derive from taking their own life. [5]* Walking away from a situation is a short-lived reprieve if you cannot open your self-awareness to see what this aggravation reflects on you. At the same time, the Universe will be alerted to provide you with another interactive opportunity with someone like the person you thought you'd just rid yourself of.

Even though the outside packaging may differ, the insides and prevailing communication dynamic will be the same. The God Force is very patient. If you didn't get the lesson the first time, God will happily help you co-create another one. It will reflect a similar

---

[5] *People who die before their natural time, and under diseased, accidental, or other similar conditions, are almost always trying to work out certain psychic conditions from which they previously suffered or died in a former lifetime. With such strong psychic impingements, such a person inevitably attracts himself to a similar condition in the present life, subconsciously hoping to conquer it. This is done repetitiously from life to life, until such a person learns to live through it. Tempus Procedium. El Cajon: Unarius Science of Life, 1965, 105*

Journey to Awakened Consciousness

scenario repeating itself until you can see it as a mirror that has been custom-made to help you become aware of your inner workings.

This discussion is based on my spiritual understanding up till now and is meant to stimulate interest in the condition of your soul. Well beyond my comprehension is Mother/Father God in charge, and I also am aware that dispensations can be given if someone takes their life for reasons known only to the God Force. Dispensation means a free pass that allows the person to bypass the customary laws regarding such an occurrence.

Time is inconsequential on the other side because it doesn't function in a linear sense as we do in the third dimension. There is no judgment if a lesson takes two days, twenty years, or several lifetimes to accomplish. To make a long story short, attempting to fix others is not only an incredible drain, but more importantly, you are not here to live anyone else's life. You can only share with them what've you learned. You will feel the power of that statement when you realize how hard it is to change yourself. It will likely be easier to speculate about what someone else should be doing than practice meditation to uncover more about yourself. Getting involved in someone else's business takes much less effort, which is why gossip has become widespread. It's an easy distraction.

Usually, groups of people or individuals will congregate to gossip because they are of like mind, or operate at a similar level of consciousness, so they take comfort in abiding by or agreeing to the same views and opinions. On the other hand, in a day of self-reckoning, an individual may find themselves taking solace in their developmental expansion. It can leave you feeling very alone, but there is no turning back once you become aware because to continue gossiping would essentially be turning on yourself, and there is no worse alone feeling than that.

There's safety in mandating what someone else should be doing since there are no personal consequences to manage, and why there

Exploring Your Humanity

is nothing more challenging than dealing with the implications of fully living your own life and every choice you make. That takes guts. To do it without numbing yourself and allow each moment to unfold, facing it head-on, requires real bravery. Using addictive behaviors, including alcohol, drugs, self-mutilation, food, sex, shopping, gambling, etc., or anything that masks the real you, only feeds insecurities.

The ego stays in a continual position to defend the *named* individual, so defenses are what you perceive around that person. Yet, the still voice within constantly urges the ego or personality to be in concert with the soul (the unlimited being). When the ego is ready to accept that soul is part of the same body, mind, and spirit and come to a peaceful agreement, the product of that union creates a remarkable power. The uplifting energy emanates like radio waves as available support for everyone.

The paradox and actual cycle of abuse are that the state of separation created within the person using the addictive behavior leads them to believe that the temporary high is healing them. The deeply wounded part of the individual being briefly anesthetized does get relief; however, it remains apart from the whole person. Repeatedly quieting the pain fosters a false belief that they are well and that there is nothing to heal, so a union of the psyche and soul never occurs. The original ache and reason to drink-drug-shop, or alter reality in any other way, will resurface once the numbing wears off because the pain was only deadened but never fully mended.

Usually, this indicates a sad heart made from lifestyle choices. The person may realize that a change is needed, but after evaluating the situation, they feel they need more gumption. Making new choices could bring up a lot of uneasiness, so they keep the old familiar thought processes in play. Suppose they choose the comfort of 'no change' to avoid feeling insecure. In that case, they may become aware that this cycle of unhappiness becomes even more

Journey to Awakened Consciousness

pronounced with the decision to remain paralyzed in their old familiar fears.

It has taken some years to embrace all I agreed to do while on Earth. Previously, I called myself stupid many times for the things I signed up for, wondering why I would do that to myself, yet it seemed I could accomplish anything while in a state of bliss floating high in the clouds. Now, I don't have to judge myself for anything and recognize that it took much love to have made such agreements, complete them all, and more.

The pat on the back inspired a pledge that I would use the same tenderness on anyone who had felt battered and beaten down, and I could also keep it gentle for myself by simply using what I've learned not to repeat past mistakes. The point was, I'd better get it right because soon I'd be dead, and then it was too late. The God I had grown up with and learned about in elementary school only gave me one chance.

My prayers bring comfort as I call forth the spiritual guides, guardians, and angels surrounding me. This is my invitation to let them know I am open to receiving suggestions on how to proceed. Although they are always there to give loving support, they only intercede by telling you what to do if you ask for their input. Even then, it comes as a gentle recommendation and will never feel like an order or controlling command. I talk silently to Mother-Father-God about all that is going on in my life as I would a best friend. I have shifted the notion of an unforgiving God waiting to punish me with a lightning bolt for making a false move into One who loves me unconditionally. This allows me to learn from my individual experiences and never refer to any of these outcomes as mistakes but instead shines a light on places I may have judged myself unfairly.

I didn't feel nearly as much like killing myself when I realized I was not a helpless victim. I felt less persecuted as I knew that others were not out to get me but just involved in their learning as they

Exploring Your Humanity

played out their perspective parts on the same stage. I began evaluating my actions and choices to see if they served me. Using the words 'serve me' helps to enable a connection with absolute authority by accessing the vibration of the soul, which will immediately bypass the fleeting inclinations of personality. If you are ever uncertain about what to do or what not to do, ask yourself, "Does it serve me?" It helps you determine if you are deciding out of obedience because it's what someone else wants you to do or if it resonates with your highest good and joy.

The caveat: if you ask if a thing is good for you, it opens the door for failure to creep in because if it doesn't work out, what's left is that it was terrible for you. Sliding back into right or wrong, good or bad, and a lightning bolt God frame of reference only ushers in the return of black-and-white thinking patterns. The equation translates into this; if I feel it's the right way, I congratulate myself. If it's the wrong way, I chastise myself and go back into the same cycle of perpetuated abuse.

I don't have to feel cheated or abandoned after making a prayer request and not seeing it manifest in an expected timeframe. This old-fashioned notion of a Santa Claus God had left many souls wondering why they were not in the lineup when joy, happiness, and abundance were passed out. Waiting for God to deliver can leave a person feeling disheartened, especially when you see others seemingly manifest everything they want while you've prayed for years, and nothing showed up! Based on this belief, you can feel unworthy and eventually lose interest in living.

I have found that embracing the concept of being a co-creator with the God Force is what inspires me. This activator gives your prayer wings and sets it in motion. Acting as if you fully believe does accentuate the vibe of a request and is also perceived by the Universe as believable. There is never an ounce of judgment on these prayer wishes. God will simply match the energy. If you send a thought out

Journey to Awakened Consciousness

on something you wish to manifest in your life with some doubt attached, then disbelief returns to you as a person or situation that reflects this lack of faith.

The Universe is highly creative, and viewing your co-creating abilities from this perspective allows you to also know that you can call forth the opposite of doubt. You can clear the original distrust anytime as it enters your thoughts by replacing it with trust. Breathe in faith, exhale doubt. Once you understand this concept, feeling superstitious is no longer necessary while waiting for the supreme deity to shine favor upon you because you've done all the right things or offered up sufficient praise.

The truth is what you believe is what you call forth. As you start fresh and know the power of your thoughts to create, you need not feel depressed or like dying, thinking God must have forgotten about you. Fortified with your new empowerment, you live and feel excited about participating as a co-creator and co-author of your book of life. The best way to show this critical teaching and Universal law is to observe how some people's belief systems *do not* serve them. The best example is when your head is full of ideas on what you need, and you miss out on the blessing that shows up instead.

Co-Create. If you know someone brokenhearted for not finding the perfect mate, you could remind them of the term co-creation. This means that as you pray for someone to love you, you also leave room for God's opinion. Just trusting that Mother-Father-God knows your heart fully and is already aware of what you yearn for will allow you to be open to what comes along. It may be a Protestant person rather than a Baptist, or a factory worker may show up rather than a Bank President. Although it may not be the person you had in mind, your heart will be soothed, not your brain. All that is required is to be open and trust in synchronicities.

Exploring Your Humanity

You can trust your decrees and know that thoughts and prayers are heard. Then, sleep soundly with the angels knowing that the Universe is excited about giving you a multitude of confirmations, both subtle and dramatic, to confirm the power of your ability to create. In addition to validating your eternal lineage, this soul power helps you remember that God's force of creation is within you, not outside you.

The most effective remedy for burnout is to take some time and focus on yourself.

You Are What You Believe & Create Accordingly
Embracing Sovereignty

    To feel worthy of love and abundance, I had to make sure I was divine from the inside out. This endeavor would include examining my strongest beliefs and ideals to see if they matched the life I chose to manifest. If there was one little thought in my head that implied being not worthy of prosperity, health, and wealth, then like a satellite dish, that is what the Universe transmitted back to me. No judgment, just the 'law of like attracts like' steadfastly delivering.

    This motivated me to tune in to any 'less than' belief systems that could interfere with me receiving the fullness of sovereign blessings, namely, my God-given right to be happy, joyous, and free. This was no easy task once awareness came to light of how everything I had been taught as a child was loitering like mental sludge, too dense to allow any new thoughts to enter. Simple teaching, like looking both ways before you cross the street, demonstrates a rote task done without thinking, suggesting how deeply etched in the psyche many of these lessons are. Well-founded or not, I became equally aware of how automatic my responses had been to the assortment of beliefs imparted to me.

    Like a good girl, I learned and adopted them as my own. The thought of questioning any of it only occurred well into my adult life. I knew these unthinking reactions had been drilled into my brain and kept the light of my soul in a semi-slumber state of being. Little ever got to shine through, and so much remained masked by the layers of

Exploring Your Humanity

rules, regulations, and beliefs created from thousands of years of humans interacting on earth.

Come to find out, the most incredible gift I'd garnered was an internal sense of peace and freedom. It seemed an impossible wall of mass consciousness to face, but if I were to claim my Sovereignty and the feeling of freedom it represented, then I must believe what God believed about me. A queen, in God's eyes, as it relates to abundance, would also mean more than acquiring material things. In that regard, I understood no one could tip or knock the crown off my head but me.

Unless I make a conscious choice to play small to avoid conflict or creatively preserve my well-being, then every other thought will require evaluation as to whether or not it reflects more masked consciousness or is an accurate portrayal of who I AM. [6]* Every decision in this new now will either be a cover-up to hide behind, playing the games accepted and practiced by the majority or risk safety and exposure by showing a true unmasked face.

Peace and freedom are the goals. I'd like to share some thoughts that hindered me from embracing my Sovereignty and how I matched each Poverty Consciousness [7]* with an abundant decree.

---

[6] *Author's Note* – Anyone unfamiliar with the term IAM may understand its meaning through the example of an apple tree loaded with fruit. The tree may have some blossoms, different color leaves, some fruit bitten into, some apples on the ground in perfect condition, and others already rotting. What's significant is that every aspect, perfect and non-perfect, melds into its entirety. And so, the concept can also be applied to being human as it relates to your IAM presence.

[7] *Author's Note* - It is poverty consciousness that beats you up with phrases like I'm not good enough, not pretty enough, too dyslexic to read, overridden with wrinkles, sagging skin, frizzy fly-away thinning hair, covered with age spots, and not smart enough. Hanging on to these words and beliefs keeps them alive and active because they draw similar frequencies of other like-minded

Journey to Awakened Consciousness

To use the word decree is crucial because it means that if you say it, it is so. In claiming, I would release all my old beliefs and open the portal of divine blessings that unintentionally stayed locked up in false ideas about my value as a human being. Whenever doubt knocks at my door, I remember that fear can no longer enslave me because God/Goddess I AM.

Old Belief: God will punish me if I make a false move or don't learn from my mistakes the first time. I get one chance to get it right because God is unforgiving and will not tolerate error.

Example: One morning, I was looking out my bedroom window and noticed a huge tree in my yard had fallen onto the neighbor's property. I quickly scanned my most recent events, wondering what I might have done to displease God that such an unpleasant thing happened.

New Decree: God loves me unconditionally and allows me to learn without judgment or recrimination at my own pace. I do not need to carry a superstitious notion of God that leaves me waiting for the other shoe to drop if I make a mistake.

Reminder: If something unfortunate happens, it is not because God is upset with me.

Old Belief: God is Masculine.

---

energies like a magnet. Every time you repeat these words, it is like making a decree that powerfully determines your health and spiritual, emotional, mental, and physical well-being. These thought forms collect and become an impasse to manifesting abundance.

Exploring Your Humanity

Example: Talking about God as HE and religious references or prayers that make God sound like a singular male aspect. My life was forever changed when my best friend Sara shared her vision of God in a near-death experience after momentarily being pronounced clinically dead. [8]*

New Decree: God is half male and half female, with individual male and female aspects that merge into one light. Mother-Father- God.

Reminder: The world has existed under male domination [9]*; however, in this new age of ascension rising, the Feminine must receive equal acclaim and honor for peace to prevail. Glory be that on a pedestal.

Old Belief: I am strong and justify being blessed by carrying your pain. I have physical, emotional, and mental strength, so I take

---

[8] *Then, as the pulling motion continued, a woman came forth and, in a very feminine voice, said, "I am the mother." The pure reverence of Catholic school training left her with startling and astonishing thoughts, "God is a woman!" And then, like that wasn't enough, a booming male voice filled the space, "and I am the father." The two merged, but surprisingly she could still see both individually even though they'd become one light. Truth with No Proof Amazon 2016 (Sara's Story, page 166)*

[9] *Understood using the old reference of He, and then groups of individuals mocking it up and holding a male child with a bit more importance. In the new now, it is all the same, for soul light can jump into male or female bodies and still be the same soul light. The one thing unalterable is the origin of your light and who or what you are. Gender cannot minimize or aggrandize you. The Voice of Ascension 2018 (IAM Jesus Christ)*

Journey to Awakened Consciousness

responsibility for your well-being since you don't empower yourself. If you are feeling downtrodden or depressed, I am not worthy of wellness either. It is only fair that I suffer along with you because if you are not okay, I am not entitled to be in a better place than you.

Example A: Having operated under the archaic belief system that says everyone else comes first made this easy. I always matched someone else's somber mood and commiserated accordingly, hoping to make the person feel better about themselves but not realizing how harmful it was to us. If I spoke on the phone to someone disgusted with their life, I didn't dare sound so happy because that didn't seem fair or the way to be a true friend. I had to stay on the same wavelength to be liked and accepted. Yet to match unhappy with more unhappy was no way to reflect the glory within.

Nobody had taught me that showing a blissful state of being to another human was a great gift because it may occur to this person one day that they might like to be and feel well too. The flip side is that if a person is choosing to remain a victim by continuing to believe they are "entitled" to help without an ounce of gratitude, clearly, they have no interest in lifting themselves, which makes it very displeasing and exhausting to try and help on any level because, for them, it is never enough.

They become experts at getting what they wish from people using drama, trauma, tears, and terror, in equal capacity if it will strengthen their cause as a victim, which keeps them from feeling the need to do anything on their own. Their philosophy is heralded in not having to bother if you can get someone to do it. Once awakened, you will catch on to this mode of operation and quickly step back, stepping in only when your chalice is full, not just because manipulation, obligation, or guilt caught you by the throat.

Example B: Regarding stepping back from my family situation, I felt the subtle thought forms of mass consciousness and replaying

Exploring Your Humanity

the same old scenarios in my mind that kept me in a state of martyrdom. I kept myself locked up in handcuffs by continually replaying these messages and believing it's never okay to detach yourself from your home and family because this is your job, and you must not quit, even if it means you suffer from the weight of it until you drop.

The problem with this Belief is that mental and emotional suffering does not count. The only proof considered valid by mass consciousness was showing that you had been physically hurt in some way before removing yourself from the situation. After jeopardizing my health to nearly breaking into pieces, I finally decided that taking action to preserve myself was justified.

Being raised in the confines of organized religion saw me adopting the concept of putting everyone else first. This was a big part of the struggle. No explanation was ever offered for the blatant discrepancies and injustices that occur in daily life, and without understanding that each person's lessons are dependent upon their unique soul agreements and past lifetime predispositions, you were only left with a haunting desperation of not being able to fix those you love from their folly.

Instead, they preach long-suffering and the selfless service necessary for lasting salvation. Therefore, no matter what illness or problem you have, as a good person, it is always meant for you to address the discomfort of others before attending to yourself.

Taking up this burden was my cross to bear. God forbid I'd ever become too powerful on my own. That would be selfish, so I felt it only fitting to give my vitality away. In addition, I have had lifetimes of being an empath and have plenty of experience in this area. This form of patterning had been an engrained experience to take away people's suffering by coveting it as my own. This tendency, along with the religious conditioning, kept me in a blind cycle of self-abuse.

Journey to Awakened Consciousness

New Decree: I am strong and can enjoy this aspect of myself without feeling the need to give it away. This is what I reflect on anyone whose path I cross +. I am worthy of wholeness and health. I never need to lessen my life force by connecting with outside discordant energy.

I give when I feel it in my heart and my cup is full. It could mean a physical gift or simply giving of my time. This giving has no resonance with special dates or holidays listed on the calendar. It comes from the soul, and it does not matter whether I gift you anonymously through prayer or in a way that everyone can see. Whether charitable contributions are made public or stay anonymous, assisting my world and those in it springs forth when the natural inclination to do so presents itself.

My responsibility is to see that I am in a state of wellness. It is not following Universal Law that I diminish myself to raise another person. My goal is not to rob another soul of a lesson. Their unique form of discomfort could be a catalyst for optimum growth and expansion one day.

Letting go of the need to save, rescue, or fix anyone, is how I permit others to face their reality. I can speak my truth based on my own experiences, which is what I have to offer. Whether the other person uplifts their condition is solely up to them. It is not my job to fix anybody. My main task is to see that my energy supply stays full, so I am healthy and balanced emotionally. I am the only one who can do that for me.

Reminder: In this dizzying energy on the planet, you must diligently guard and protect your energy supply. One phone call that goes on too long could be enough to drain your last bit of reserve. Hold your energy tank sacred. Otherwise, you can become depleted, making your immune system vulnerable and get run down physically. If I fall back into suffering because someone I

Exploring Your Humanity

love is suffering, I will remember being created to be happy, joyous, free, and worthy.

Old Belief: I cannot look too good because it will upset people and stir jealousy. Being proud of my physical beauty is also unfair because some people may not have it, which wouldn't be considerate. Therefore, I never look my best to ensure I am accepted, stay safe, and keep the peace. It's always best to tone myself down whenever possible to fit in by not making waves.

Example: Any time I find myself adjusting my looks, personality, or demeanor to suit someone other than myself.

New Decree: I will not mold myself into someone else's version of how I am to be and look. Better to hear a few whispers under someone's breath or catch a few stares of disapproval than suffer the slavery of marching to anyone else's beat. Today, I pay attention, especially if I am trying to shrink by hiding my abilities or altering my appearance to avoid appearing as full of myself. Majestic order indicates me being all I can be, and if that displays a purple top, yellow pants, and multi-colored shoes, then so be it.

Reminder: What anyone else thinks of me is irrelevant and none of my business. Gossip is a problem if you emphasize what people say about you because, in doing so, you are opening yourself to the influences of the vibrations of those consciousnesses.

Regarding the disappointment of rampant gossip, Mother-Father-God has given me a few words to gain understanding; "Many daughters, sisters, and brothers alike have counterparts raging a war within them." It softened the hurt because knowing its duality makes the reason for gossip understandable without judging anyone for participating. The opposites within each person seem to attack each

Journey to Awakened Consciousness

other and only leave the chaos of no center point or balance, which is how you feel if you take gossip to heart.

Old Belief: I must look good by dying and styling my hair, be the proper weight, and wear makeup to match what's trending.

Example: I just wanted to feel better; however, changing my hair color didn't do the trick. At sixty-something, I decided to let my silver-gray hair come through and stopped dying it. A head full of bright shiny silver hair was appealing to me, and so it was. The silver was now a year old and looking great until I heard a little girl whisper to her mother in the airport restroom that I looked like her grandmother. Vanity set in, and the salt-and-pepper hair growth wasn't good anymore.

On my next trip to the market, I saw a box of metallic silver hair dye on the shelf, and the model looked stunning. My better judgment screamed *don't do it*, I had to do it anyway. I wanted to see what the metallic would do to my silvery hair. I needed a perk and did not consider that seventy-five percent of my head was a dark brunette when it clearly read on the box that said color was for blonde or medium blonde hair.

None of it seemed to matter. My mind was made up. Went ahead with it. After washing was shocked to see that my lovely hair was now a taupe shape of baby puke and duller than dull. I couldn't muster up self-hate at that point and was dearly disappointed. Self-acceptance teetered on the brink of some serious name-calling.

New Decree: *Focus on marrying self rather than peroxide and hair color.* It seemed impossible because, after this last escapade, I insisted on a separation. Horrible as it sounded, I would always return to

Exploring Your Humanity

myself, and even if I threatened divorce, the ultimatum was short-lived because if I didn't want me, then what. My bestie stepped up by suggesting that it was the Universe's way of letting me know I looked fine the way I was, naturally. Ah, the love of a best friend.

Reminder: Focus on happiness. Ascension is the timeless moment when you allow everything to blend, removing any judgment of right or wrong, good or bad, beautiful or ugly, and placing yourself in neutral gear, leaving any final determinations on anything to God. The Ascended State is the place that defines nothing. A place where labels disappear and all energies are considered a divine part of learning. *Eternal youth and beauty* are part of that God-Like consciousness that never ages because it remains untouched by human judgment, causing no ripples on the timeline.

Old Belief: I cannot be authentic because my personality can be wild, loud, and outrageous. This could be misconstrued as showing off, or people might think something is wrong with me if I act too outrageous and have too much fun.

Example: I have lots of energy and often want to jump into conversations to entertain and make people laugh. There is a natural urge within me to always want to kick things up a notch and accelerate any energy that is too quiet or staid. Growing up in church every Sunday proved problematic as I'd encounter glaring stares that implied something was seriously wrong with me. Not wanting to create suspicion about being high on drugs or alcohol, I quickly learned not to attract such attention because it would take a long time to prove my sobriety and that I was not possessed, suffering from mental illness or a personality disorder.

New Decree: It is okay for me to be who I AM. That is how I honor myself. The urge to sing, dance, yell, breathe loudly, or talk in a cartoon voice is perfectly acceptable when alone. I can enjoy feeling a surge of energy moving thru me that instigates a flare-up of this behavior and the perks of being invited places because people feel entertained in my company. Those who know me claim my huge energy bursts directly correlate to the amount of sugar or food I've consumed, but in my heart, I know it's just me being me. Once a court jester, always a court jester.

Reminder: Pushing down the real me causes constipation by detaching the flow of chi from the natural spring of energy that radiates from my soul. This blockage can manifest in physical aches and complaints in places where energy circuits are restrained. Being free, I can appreciate everyone else's spiritual gifts and unique expressions of freedom without envy, jealousy, or resentment from never having honored or accepted my own.

Old Belief: My imagination feels like a curse from which I cannot escape.

Example: Some people get paid handsomely for using their imaginative abilities, but not me, all of my creativity gets spent on dreaming up trips all over the world and then enduring last-minute cancellations once it's dawned that the prospective arrangement has nothing to do with reality. I'd be convinced my imagination told me it was the 'in harmony' thing to do. In addition to that, I did have a penchant for telling and embellishing stories.

In grade school, I'd told my friends on the way home from school one Monday that my family had visited the zoo over the weekend, and I was lucky to be at school at all, considering a lion had bitten off my head. Once I told them the doctors got it and

Exploring Your Humanity

sewed it back on again, it all appeared half believable until they came to hear my mother's version of the story, which turned out to be rather embarrassing. After all, I knew it wasn't accurate to be banded as a habitual liar, but it took some fifty years to figure out I just wanted to entertain people and give them a bit of zip by adding some zest to their daily lives.

New Decree: I accept my imagination as an asset because it allows me to add color and fun to my life and the lives of others. I use my powers of imagination to bring cheer and laughter. In accepting my imagination as a gift, I honor its presence by also understanding the difference between when that aspect is choosing a little joy and reality as it pertains to making life choices in 3D.

Reminder: I don't have to be held prisoner by my highly active imagination, but I can see it as a form of self-preservation instead. My visions may be hyper-extensions of the imaginary and are just there because....and sometimes they are not. It is always a surprise when they come to fruition but accepting them as they are without expectation is helpful. It's true that conjuring up wild schemes [10]* led me to believe things that were not necessarily in my best interest, a thought of magic now and then to elaborate upon can incite sparks of electricity in the body. This vibration enlivens a sense of hope after the burnout that can occur from everyday stresses. Fairytale or

---

[10] *Author's Note: Our captivation with Greek mythology might simply be a way for mankind to review, learn, experiment, and enjoy without risking their journey. A far-reaching and grand stretch of the imagination, even harsh according to today's standards, these teachings were meant to appeal to the emotional nature of a human being, as shown in many varied instances of relationship dramas.*

Journey to Awakened Consciousness

not, the small glimmer of imagination fascinates as an asset to the wellness of body-mind-spirit surviving 3D consciousness.

Old Belief: Having a job that I dislike is a good thing. A job that causes stress or brain-rotting boredom should be acceptable because it gives my life meaning. That way, I can feel suffering and deduce it must be a worthwhile job, even hating it at times, for it to have any value. Commiserating with others who were miserable in their careers was a part of that too. Sharing in the job grief and dissatisfaction made this bonding process feel like a worthwhile experience.

Example A: One day years ago, I was leaving my 9 to 5 job on a Friday afternoon, looking forward to the weekend. On the way to the car, I thought it was a miserable week because I was not too fond of work, but that must mean that sticking it out is valuable and worthwhile. What an attention grabber. It made me aware that much of my life had been lived by following someone else's code of monotonous standards.

Example B: There have been times when I've had to make significant changes to live within my means, like the time my first choice was to live in an area where rents were highly-priced, but after many years of the same job, it felt too stressful to only work to pay rent. In addition, I found it difficult to put a price on opening my heart and utilizing my spiritual abilities for gain. At a time of so much uncertainty and fear regarding health and money concerns for others, it did not feel in sync to charge money for sessions.

Life was in constant flux, and due to the erratic nature of things on the planet, it was a challenge to tune into anything but the present moment. People always had the standard queries about money, love,

Exploring Your Humanity

and job security. I had always received helpful guidance for clients, but I could only get an answer if one were there, making the idea of putting a dollar value on the service nearly impossible. Not to mention, in my case, you may not even get paid!

What comes to mind is a lady who felt dissatisfied with her appointment because I could not answer her primary question, which was to know when her ex-husband would die. What? It may be an extreme example, but she was upset he owed her money and was waiting for him to die. His death, according to her, was the only thing that would assure her the proper funding. I was shocked by her audacity but would never even attempt to answer such a query under any circumstance, nor have I been privy to receiving such information. (That I know of)

The other unanswered question was about an elevator company she was suing. She was on the third floor of a building and returning to the lobby when a severe mechanical malfunction dropped the car at high speed to ground level, leaving her top teeth slamming down on the bottom ones. It was challenging to focus on anything after hearing that, I tried, yet all I seemed to notice was the silhouetted illusion of jagged mountain peaks just below her gum line. Not much left of those top teeth, and it didn't help things much when I found myself completely unable to offer any pearls of wisdom on why she was not making a fortune off the incident.

She had seemed so unhappy upon arrival that I had made an extra effort to lift her spirits, so it was disappointing that she refused to pay for the hour. Interestingly, my caring emotions quickly took on a provoked tone after hearing the explanation of why she chose to snub me, and upon handing her the cassette tape recording of our time together, I curtly replied, "Take your unhappy self and go from here." Nothing like that had ever happened before, so I was stunned and shaken, especially since I needed to steady myself for another client waiting in the courtyard outside my office.

Journey to Awakened Consciousness

The issue often arose because it never felt right to charge money for my abilities. I began the work nineteen years earlier, charging only $15 for an hour, which was near over the top of what I could accept from an ethical standpoint. It is an excellent example of feeling poorly about receiving payment to answer questions, especially when you never know what someone might ask of you.

New Decree: I am worthy of having a job that I am comfortable doing. It is Sovereign to receive money or any other energy exchange in return for your work, no matter what, and to feel the joy of finding a mutual balance. Only I can dare to follow my passion, even in a society that wants to define the profession you choose thru ratings. The highest is a doctor or lawyer, and the lowest is a ditch digger or tarot card reader. In the Universal scheme of things, it isn't for anyone to say which is better or worse. It is my divine right to accept money for a job I feel happy and uplifted doing.

Reminder: Everyone has a right to make a living at their chosen form of employment. I came to terms with it back then under the guise that what I was charging for was my time. Money is a societal element and custom in which people monitor their progress. Still, I couldn't put a price on my work that matched the output of energy I'd facilitate, so it fell out of joy.

My passion shifted from doing one-on-one in-person sessions to sitting alone and focusing my abilities on writing books to offer guidance with no income. There is no price for freedom, and if living in an affordable place meant having to bypass the top choice, then so be it, it was what I had to do to be free of stress. Without self-love-aligned thinking, it was another setup for feeling isolated since I alone could give value to my work and claim self-worth accordingly.

Exploring Your Humanity

Old Belief: *I can't win* or take a win on anything.

Example: Whenever things didn't go to plan, or there was difficulty in executing even the simplest of tasks, I would feel frustrated and utter, *I can't win*. Sometimes there would be discord in attempting to communicate feelings to someone and feeling defeated from that effort, silently whispering the exact same words. It got my attention how often I said, *I can't win*. I'd spend hours on end and much unnecessary time worrying about why someone didn't get me, why they didn't understand, or even why they still didn't understand when I did explain. What a hellish nightmare and lack of freedom I'd unknowingly created for myself.

New Decree: In this new now, I don't minimize myself by feeling the need to explain anything to anyone unless I feel a natural desire to do so. Understanding I've spent a lifetime waiting for validation from the outside world helped me realize I was headed toward spiritual bankruptcy from constantly being in the motion of having to scan for where to deposit time and energy to receive a receipt of self-worth in return.

As an awakened being, I became conscious that I was calling forth a negative experience each time I said, *'I can't win.'* Being aware can turn it into a positive experience because you hold sacred the mighty powers of creation and choice to create anew at any moment. We all have probably, at one time or another, based our self-worth on how much others needed us; however, I win each time I dig deeper into my inner place where I value myself, I like myself, and I am enough.

Reminder: *I don't seem able to take a win on anything* expression had to shift with the revelation that repeating win-lose verbiage, as such, was a setup for defeat and depression. Reinforcing that philosophy suggested no options, only the black-and-white world of success or failure. It became too extreme to say; *I can't win*.

Journey to Awakened Consciousness

Old Belief: Anytime something wonderful happened, I couldn't accept it because it left me with the nagging feeling that something terrible would show up to justify the good. I was always waiting for the other shoe to drop. To have any wealth, I must first experience something considered *less than*, so it wouldn't be too noticeable that I was receiving goodness and blessings from the Universe without first enduring hardships. When I was fortunate enough to receive some good thing, the old Belief translated a familiar equation… Suffering+ more suffering = it is finally okay to obtain a little prosperity. Good fortune had to do with forces outside of my control.

Example 1: This may sound strange, but I couldn't feel excited about going on vacation for the longest time because I always anticipated an impending disaster. I did not feel deserving of any satisfying fulfillment, so something terrible had to happen before the trip to offset any happiness coming my way. Although some of these thought forms might have come from other lifetimes, I was acutely aware of how the idea of limited abundance was kept in play. Someone once said to me, "Who do you think you are to get to go away so often?"

This statement reminded me of my worst fear: I wasn't worthy of such pleasure. The irony is that it turned out to be a poignant gift because it activated a reason to look beyond the initial upset and hurt from hearing these words. It's always a choice whether I take what's being said to me as an insult or look deeper into myself to ascertain what's causing the upset. Anytime I react strongly, I've learned the finger always points back to me and my false beliefs.

Example 2: I moved in with a very dear friend who was struggling with his sales position. Shortly after I arrived, he got two

Exploring Your Humanity

great leads and was so happy he thought I must have brought him good luck. He was so convinced, with a sense of humor he said he would tie me to a chair if I ever thought about leaving. I reminded him that he had been doing a morning and evening meditation to call forth abundance. Still, he was so set on it coming from a *force outside himself* that he couldn't connect it to the power he had already set in motion due to his daily prayer and light work. Like so many people, he was intent on believing that all good fortune is due to luck or the result of some superstitious belief. [11]*

New Decree: My abundance is delivered and disbursed according to my beliefs about receiving. How I command and call it forth is entirely up to me. There is no *less than* energy lurking, and the flow of wealth is simply there for the claiming. The trips and travel are bountiful simply because my greatest joy is being matched with more joy. I receive happy opportunities without reservation to honor their presence in my life.

Reminder: I am here to experience unlimitedness in the illusion of limitedness.

Old Belief: I need to do something else to busy myself when sitting down and enjoying food.

Example: After preparing a meal, I look around to ensure everything has been cleaned up instead of just sitting down to eat. I'm not content to enjoy the food but become the cleanup queen. I

---

[11] *Human thought creates what it imagines; the phantoms of superstition project their real deformity in the Astral Light and live by the very terrors they produce. They owe their being to the delusions of imagination and the aberration of the senses. They are never produced in the presence of anyone who knows and can expose the mystery of their monstrous birth." The law of Psychic Phenomena'*

Journey to Awakened Consciousness

will also do cleaning tasks, sort and open mail, make a grocery list, talk on the phone, and even do laundry while eating.

New Decree: I can nourish myself by taking the time to eat without interruptions. I sit quietly and enjoy every bite as I give thanks for the nourishment and physical healing.

Reminder: My body is the sacred vessel for my soul. I will treat it accordingly.

Old Belief: I need to feel in control of everything because it is too scary to trust and believe that things work out for the best. Divine timing never seems to come soon enough, so I hold myself in check and monitor every move and breath. I cannot relax enough to be in the **now** moment because I'm too worried about what's ahead and won't be ready for what's coming.

Example: I planned to visit England and Ireland on one of my trips overseas. Never having been to Ireland, I spent much time mapping out locations and accommodations. It turns out that I never used those plans. Shortly after arriving in England, I met a man and woman sitting on a park bench. In our brief conversation, they told me about their visit to the Roslin Chapel outside of Edinburgh, Scotland, and that I should consider visiting this sacred place. To make a long story short, I took their advice, fell in love with the area, and ended up reconnecting with old familiar soul mates who have since become friends for life. I will always be grateful I was able to put my original plans aside to receive such a surprise.

New Decree: I understand that the need to have a plan, moment to moment, keeps the illusion of control a primary force. I do not need to analyze every project detail beforehand and can trust that the Universe will guide me if I stay open-minded.

Exploring Your Humanity

Reminder: Being open to each time frame in the present allows me to overcome the controlling impulse of impatience and experience peace because six seconds ago is unchangeable history, and five minutes from now is the unknown, creating speculation. Being in the now sets me free from expectations, simplifies my life, and lets me enjoy what occurs in the present moment; when I expect something, the frustration and anxiety of waiting for it to develop overrides anything else that shows up in the interim instead. A helpful lesson given to me by my master guide gave me relief: "Expect nothing and receive all things."

Old Belief: I am not choosing to go through more traumatic emotional processes. I feel tired of crying and the fragility of being vulnerable. I feel angry because it never seems to be finished.
Example: I was exhausted from weeping and processing. Like the endless tears falling from peeling an onion, there was no relief. I didn't want to feel that fragile and couldn't tolerate the feeling of raw exposure any longer; I would get angry instead.
New Decree: Part of gaining mastery is accepting my human condition and allowing for the susceptibility that goes along with it. In moments of helplessness, I trust that I will not wither away from feeling fragile, knowing that God supports me.
Reminder: Determine what you are angry about, then give it your full attention. Just under the surface emotion of anger is pure fear, so the secret is not to ignore it. Once it merges within you, that high-intensity emotion will no longer feel the need to scream, rage, or cry for your attention. As a complete universe, you form a full circle by letting any emotion stay long enough to recognize why it is there. The answer to your anger is within, and it will not be balanced

Journey to Awakened Consciousness

by directing it outward or trying to cover it up with self-defeating habits or addictive behavior.

Old Belief: It is someone else's job to see that I am feeling happy and fulfilled.

Example: Marrying my husband convinced me it was his job to care for me in all ways, including getting me the perfect job, helping me find the right friends, the best hobbies, etc. He made it easy for me to accept his caretaking because he immensely enjoyed playing the caretaker role. What an education, especially when it got to the place where I didn't feel he was doing a good enough job. It left me with an underlying resentment and affected my capacity to love him fully.

New Decree: I am responsible for my happiness and do not just fall into unfortunate or unlucky circumstances. I know everything is agreed upon, or it wouldn't happen. There are no mistakes. I decided on the relationship dynamics I'd be part of and the fullness of all it has taught me and all I have offered in return. When I got in touch with this concept of relationships being called forth and agreed upon, the need to qualify who is right or wrong subsided, and the focus of looking at what is being reflected took precedence. This is so I can learn how to take care of myself.

Reminder: Resentment is the weed that chokes the life force out of love. It takes root when the need to be taken care of gets delegated to someone else. In other words, I don't have what I want, and it's your fault for not getting it. Keeping someone responsible for my well-being and happiness was a sure way to stay in the old recycling mode. The old ways have been recycled enough. I can release expectations of someone else being accountable for my overall

Exploring Your Humanity

welfare, which frees up my body, mind, and spiritual energies to fully love myself and others.

Letting go allows the person to release resentment because you've demanded perfection from them. You, in turn, let go of any resentment you have toward them for not living up to your expectations. I remember past confirmations when a person has psychically sensed being released from my expectations of them (removed the unseen mental shackles of non-freedom) and quietly confirmed my efforts by approaching me in our subsequent communication with apparent ease.

Old Belief: I need to be very careful about what, when, where, and how I speak due to worry about how someone might interpret my words or what they may think of me because of what I say or don't say, fearing the possibility they will draw false conclusions about who I am.

Example A: This hypervigilance came about from an inability to express feelings that genuinely matched what I wished to convey about myself. The matter was compounded by continually rehearsing what to say, thinking if I practiced often, I could deliver excellent communication for someone to understand without confusion. I rehearsed often, but each rehearsal left me feeling more insecure than when I started. As the frustration mounted, telling a little white story came into play because telling the truth can feel quite blunt, so it seemed much easier to match what people expected to hear rather than risking you'd create discord by speaking your truth.

Example B: When someone asks, for example, "How are you?" I assumed they genuinely wanted to know and answered accordingly. However, picking and choosing words to respond to the simple question took a lot of work. It became a lot easier when my dear mother alerted me that most people are just being polite when they ask that question but are not necessarily interested in what's going on or the specific details.

New Decree: I can speak my truth by intending to do so without being hurtful or harmful to anyone or anything. I never have expectations of how anyone will perceive my words. Live and let live.

Reminder: Anytime I adjust communication because of what someone else will think, I pause, knowing nothing is worse for the body than carrying around a load of resentment and anger because I diminished myself.

An exception to this rule would be when a choice is made to adjust words in a conversation to avoid unnecessary conflict, which remains my God-given right to exercise free will in that form. Being conscious of the power you hold within verbiage allows you the space of a neutral zone, where you are clear on having the prerogative to play with words as you choose.

With practice and awareness, you can also identify any events of the past where unspoken words may be causing clutter, so to acknowledge them allows for their clearance and presents a new opportunity for a clean bill of emotional health, leaving no extra energy build up in the throat chakra or physical body.

Old Belief: I'm an important person.

Example: My pride is easily injured, and I feel embarrassed if something doesn't go according to the status quo and others observe or know about it.

New Decree: On my own, I am tiny, like an ant, one in millions scurrying about; however, in unison with Mother-Father- God, I am everything.

Exploring Your Humanity

Reminder: I used to think I knew it all, but life's experiences have humbled me, and all I know now is what I've learned from living life. All the fuss over what other people believe means nothing because no one has the authority to define me, only God knows who I am, and that is good enough.

In place of this statement, if I act like you in your company or with anyone else, that is only me playing. If I ever feel truly safe, you may see and feel the real authentic me. Otherwise, I am just playing. If I ever worry about what someone thinks, I remember no one cares about the trivial things my ego has blown up. Most people are consumed in their own lives and have no genuine interest in mine other than making me the distraction of an impertinent gossip session. This truth isn't to minimize anyone but to alleviate unnecessary anxiety.

Old Belief: I am lazy if I feel like sitting around and doing nothing for hours.

Example: I must always be doing something to feel good. This might include buying something, rearranging furniture, clearing out old things, starting a new project, cleaning, or helping someone else. I become extremely restless and feel unworthy if I am not in doing mode.

New Decree: Whatever I do or don't do is no measure of my value as a human being. It was plentiful simply to have taken my first breath on earth and come into human form as someone who fully loves God and Planet Earth.

Reminder: Another of my master guide's gems: God loves me the same whether I lay on the couch all day or busy myself from morning till night.

Journey to Awakened Consciousness

Old Belief: My great need for alone time is considered by some people to be a form of isolation. I must explain so they understand the reasons without labeling me a hermit.

Example: The essence of it was controversial because expressing my preference to be alone also included that I enjoyed company if I started to feel lonely. Hence, telling this dichotomy accurately as a full-picture representation felt like torture. The words would cascade in obscure fragments sputtering like the flow of an abandoned faucet. I would say too much or too little in an utterly innocuous attempt to communicate and end up arousing suspicion.

I might ramble, giving way too much information and overboard for what the question warranted, making me look like I was trying to defend myself, or conversely, say way too little, appearing like I was trying to hide something. I could see myself in this trouble any place or time a question was asked. Even standard queries a friend, family member, acquaintance, or professional person might ask became an opportunity for scrabble.

New Decree: The goal was to make peace with this personality aspect without explaining it to anyone.

Reminder: The one thing I indeed could never explain was the tremendous amount of alone time I needed. That is when I felt my best, always been that way. I love connecting with others, enjoying their company, and then retreating to the cave, which has always done right by me.

To create a scenario fostering an energy-free platform to enjoy space and time, one had to be highly creative. If truth be told about wishing to be alone, nobody could accept it anyway since, for most people, it was based on what made sense to them instead, so their

Exploring Your Humanity

boundless assumptions would further restrict, making the telling of a white story a must now and then.

You can imagine how I felt one day when a friend saw fit to corner me in her kitchen and ask why I didn't like her and if that was why I spent so much time away. Gasp. Smack dabbed up close and personal, my worst fear monster. The flood of having to explain came to fruition. Horror. To keep it simple and by nothing less than a miracle, I managed to let her know that it wasn't because I didn't like her, but I left the area long ago because I simply needed to search out and find like-minded metaphysical people. That momentarily quelled the thick qualm as the elephant in the room managed to escape.

The reality of this underlying subculture made it a challenge to augment the truth about myself because this living, breathing consciousness whispered, *you don't like us, so you better find a way to make it up or prove us wrong if you wish to be loved in return.* Ever present, this not very subtle reminder pervaded my mind space with its message of insinuation about those who dare to do things differently. This booming, formidable voice could affect every choice made if not recognized. A suffocating blanket backed by generations of time representing obligatory gestures at best, and if you yield to being wrapped up in it, you could fall prey to many other states of non- freedom too.

In other words, wishing for human love and bonding puts you at risk of bending over backward to please others, but in many instances, no matter how hard you try, you can never really make it right. Any compensation only leaves you vulnerable as you try to match someone else's expectations of you. After such a backbreaking and exhaustive effort to tell your truth, you eventually lose the incentive to try. In surrender, you come to a place of being okay with who and what you are, understanding you were never required to explain anything.

Journey to Awakened Consciousness

There within is the healing. At some point within those parameters was me accepting who and what I was, for good or bad, better or worse, and through sickness and in health, Me, for the long haul. This might sound easy, but no, it was not. Being *married to self* is hard work, much more complex than any other relationship I'd known or been a part of. I could accept others' misdeeds and faults more readily than face my own. You know it's not helpful to criticize anyone else, but the thought doesn't register for extending the same act of compassion toward yourself.

Once awakened, you realize that *till death do you part* may be a reality if you don't align your body, mind, and spirit because the body can only endure so much discord before it manifests illnesses. Being awakened entitles you to banish death once and for all as you stay focused on merging all aspects of your being with Mother-Father-God. I AM reminded that it is a journey of self-love first and foremost. Without that, it's just a repeat of thousands of years of walking in human shoes, just a different set of circumstances, and I, for one, am not choosing to repeat another cycle here.

To awaken is to spend less time being concerned about what others are doing, which frees up your energy, emotions, and mental space for I AM to reside in the physical body in freedom. An awakened being is not emotionally dependent upon another person's response to give them a sense of well-being but instead speaks their truth to stay aligned and in tune with self.

Old Belief: I need to numb myself with drink, drugs, food, shopping, sex, or any temporary feel-good measure to face the world without as much emotional pain.

Example: I can share an example of alcohol not working in the push-pull of personality and soul. I had been invited to a wedding

Exploring Your Humanity

reception which I was excited about attending. I wished to be a well-behaved average person with integrity, promising myself I'd only have two glasses of wine. Right. It was like telling the sun not to rise in the morning. There was an emotional current with the groom due to a prior relationship matter that I wished to remain civil over.

My well-meaning plan fell through the bottom of more than a few glasses of vino, and then after leaving the party in a blackout, I got lost in a cul-de-sac, barely making it home. Checking the fender of my car the following morning to make sure I hadn't hit anything or anyone left me feeling spiritually bankrupt.

New Decree: I can verbalize what I share without inhibiting my voice or restricting emotions by silencing myself with alcohol. Attending group rehab meetings allowed me to right this situation and served me extensively for eight years. I am incredibly grateful to the organization and affiliated people.

Reminder: I don't have to drink to have fun or be in a happy place. It feels good to face any situation soberly and boosts self-worth and self-esteem. It's very freeing to wake up in the morning and remember what I did the night before, who I talked to, and how I got back home.

Old Belief: It's never okay to change my mind once I've committed to someone or something.

Example: Sometime between eight and nine years of attending meetings to stay sober, I noticed a distinct change in how I felt. After all those years of abiding by the tenants and principles laid down by the founder, I had come to a place of liberation and felt very whole. The fear that kept me sober, though, was now the same fear that was causing anxiety and un-comfortability. It was a

Journey to Awakened Consciousness

paradox, but considering that all life is based on opposites, it made sense. In my early years, I'd walk away from a meeting feeling empowered and so thankful I had a place to share the upsetting things I used to drink over. What got my attention years later was that I was walking away from the gathering, feeling much worse than when I got there. I realized I'd been staying out of fear. Then, repeating, "Hello, my name is ___, and *I am* an alcoholic," was like bathing in the energy of alcoholic drinking every time I said it. Branding myself with that qualification each time I wanted to share with the group started to feel restrictive. Important here to remember the power of an I AM Decree, the premise being when you state it, I am_____I am _____, you are decreeing it to be fact, you make it a reality.

New Decree: My truth stands on its merit, and I can allow for the recognition that anytime I am tuning into fear-based ideas and then grappling for hours afterward to release its clutches from around my neck, I can permit myself to walk away from the situation. It is never sovereign to walk around reacting out of fear or to use fear as a motive for participation.

Reminder: I continue practicing the self-care techniques suggested for recovery and continually learn more about aspects of myself that had gotten dispersed. Having worked the program's basic tenants to the point where they were now working for me, I did not feel the need to enforce them like attending church every Sunday. They were active inside me like a tree rooted solidly in the earth.

I could live the principles because I fully embraced what I learned about myself and wove that self-knowledge onto my tapestry. It was a part of my core that could no longer be unraveled, not to mention being consciously aware of the power and vibration of words used to describe oneself!

Exploring Your Humanity

In this time of ascension, I acknowledge that I am responsible for every time I have walked upon the earth. Our greatest challenge is never about what other people do but rather about how we emotionally react or respond to their actions.

Identifying beliefs that trigger negative thinking or self-defeating behavior gives us a better chance to respond calmly rather than having <u>a knee-jerk reaction</u> to something because a repressed emotion lurking in the shadows gets activated and takes over. <u>This happens if an aspect or Belief stays unidentified by you, which keeps it reactive</u>. Being able to respond garners a sense of personal peace and nurtures peaceful interactions with everyone else.

My natural impulses are enough to affect and direct my life choices in a way that will bring about my highest joy. Anytime a debilitating Old Belief charges through my mind like a runaway train, I pause, acknowledge it as the old way, and confirm that I AM love in its presence.

Love embraces the slavery of non-freedom and reminds me that I am worthy of all the love and abundance the Universe holds sacred for me. I let the old-tattered cloak upon my shoulders that represents all the limited ways I have viewed myself and anyone else fall to the ground. As I have claimed my right to Sovereignty, I can feel everyone else's potential zoom toward awakening.

Self-Respect vs. Masked Consciousness Demands

In truth, please yourself. It's a solo journey, as succinctly said in the *Bhagavad Gita*, relating to the experience of Arjun, the warrior. The journey to wholeness refers to how we have branched outside of our true core due to free will choices, with the message being: only you can initiate the process of straightening yourself out.

Being awakened can feel like a daily battle with mass consciousness. Hopefully, more will wake up, but until then, this unseen creature makes demands of you every day. The guidelines on how you should be, act, speak, and appear all fall within the boundaries of non-freedom in its subculture of brainwashing. Standing up to it all and maintaining your spiritual integrity requires astute awareness, or you could unknowingly slip into the massive void of expectation. No wonder you may have felt exhausted.

Speaking the truth doesn't change the fact that you may feel separate from others, but there is no grander feeling of isolation than when you abandon yourself and have only spoken words to appease others. After a lifetime of calculating what to say, when to say it, and who to say it to, in addition to contriving stories and paragraphs of words to justify your right to be and breathe, the process of your awakening shines through because once personality and soul merge, the verbiage just pours out like liquid gold.

It is perfect and matches your insides so accurately it may take your breath away in awe. It's so amazing you may find yourself repeating the instance in your mind in a sort of magical disbelief that, without rehearsing, such fluid silk came from you.

Exploring Your Humanity

Don't get me wrong, I am very grateful for every bit I've invested in my development, but it leaves me stunned that it took some sixty years to achieve the marriage of self. As a human being in motion and a work in progress, I cannot shorten the time spent belaboring over words. It is understandable why anyone would choose to remain in deep slumber because it is much easier to do what is expected of you and honor the ole games of guilt and obligation rather than take a chance of being ostracized by family or friends for not following suit. What a terrible feeling to be cast out, hence, why many will prefer to dwell in societal and religious consciousness set up to rule and govern for full acceptance by all.

An irreplaceable element to the journey is knowing that you made it easier for someone else in the light of all subconscious minds being connected. In recovery mode, you understand you may have a thought that produces a feeling of guilt or obligation. You're just not held prisoner to it. To awaken is also knowing if someone chose the awakened state and didn't have to suffer or feel anguish as long it's a bonus to the personal freedom you attain.

The worst aloneness is having a false perception about yourself. No one wants to feel alone or separated, but I have often felt alone, even when surrounded by people. It doesn't get lonelier than that because if someone disapproves of you, it is a set-up within your ego to get angry and fight back with the insinuation it is the other person's job to make you feel okay. When that person does not do their job by your standards, you feel angry and resentful, which only promotes more aloneness.

Feeling a further state of separation, your chances for peace are greatly diminished because your belief suggests that you need others' approval to feel validated and worthy. What a roller coaster ride that turns out to be because you are the only person who can deem you worthy. It was put plainly and simply for me to understand when my

Journey to Awakened Consciousness

guide said, "If you base everything on fame (or lack of) and your career, you will feel poorly."

Live and learn we must; if the journey gets you to the point of self-love and acceptance, then you're awakened. You appreciate anyone sharing true feelings because it narrows the alone abyss into the spirit of human comradery and compassion. It seldom happens, though. Most have learned to disguise their truth and or tuck away their true feelings out of self-preservation or the fear of being excluded. We all will dip into that jar on occasion for momentary comfort. Yet, many will stay unaware and in slumber as they continue to immerse themselves in the old game-playing cover-ups out of habit and a false sense of security.

For example, when you are in a situation but unsure if you've done something wrong and wish to keep things as status quo, regardless of how you feel, just immediately say *sorry*, so right or wrong, you've covered yourself. Understandably, for those who remain in slumber, it's the art of hiding behind a response recognized as one of society's appropriate things to say. An asleep being wouldn't risk telling their truth, so they stick with the correct and proper answers deemed socially correct to remain in the safe zone.

We are all here having a human journey, and all you have is your experience to speak about. Hearing someone's truth is refreshing and nurtures the bonding that eludes the deepest kind of solitary pain. The place where someone trusts you enough to share their true thoughts and the resonance you feel evokes a genuine urge to affectionately hug and hold sacred the bearer. The expansion balances all that until you reach a complete acceptance, although it doesn't mean you won't shed a few tears.

Choosing self-respect can leave a sense of seclusion. There are many instances of connecting with someone during your life and finding the communication you share with that person is complete. In some cases, this can take all of five minutes and, for some, many

Exploring Your Humanity

years of ongoing contact. You can extend those interactions beyond completion if you feel obligated or guilt-ridden and then maintain a level of communication that feels more acceptable. However, you'll feel the back pedal of consequences dealing with someone who pulls you back into the ring using tears and terror with equal facility.

If you honor yourself and take the completion, the sad thing is, most often, those on the other end don't understand and will feel abandoned or deserted by you and disappointed. If you feel the heart-fullness, the hurtfulness pains because there is no way to explain or expect anyone else to understand why you call or don't, why you visit or don't, when, why, and at what intervals, etc. Come to find out, it's a full-time job just to understand your own actions and motives.

You cannot explain from an asleep consciousness modality because a silent unheard version of love is unacceptable. It does nothing and is idle, so basically, in this society considered worthless. If you place yourself within that measure, you are more isolated. How many people have said, "Oh, don't worry about calling me. Love is enough" The only one who ever shared it with me was Ascended Master Kuthumi, in the book *Love is Enough.* [12]* I hold it

---

[12] *It takes courage to be an actualized person attuned to your inner workings, your soul. Opportunities will always present to step out of that place. For example, we've noticed when people love, they insist the way to show the appropriate amount of gratitude is through doing and accommodating. Of course, the person on the giving end may have no awareness that their giving comes with certain conditions and is, to some degree, based on expectations they hold about rightfully receiving something in return. This could leave you feeling hesitant about ever receiving or accepting anything from anyone again.*

This is motivated by a subtle fear, where a part of you believes that you could be rejected if you don't acquiesce and that great offense might be taken to you insisting on doing things your way. Or dare you to say no to a personal request, and you will likely be labeled ungrateful. It takes courage to stand your ground and BE who you are, accepting things offered as they are, and

Journey to Awakened Consciousness

dear to my heart and remember I must be full of self-love and forgiveness to extend it outward. Then, on the other hand, a master guide helps you avoid the pitfalls of your brainwashed personality to be in the Soul Light you came to express.

Knowing love is enough can be challenging because if you say no to people's requests of you, it may incur a rath of unpleasant thought forms when the subsequent vibes of selfishness rain upon your energy field. What could be worse than being referred to as someone selfish. That is the translation when someone doesn't have a self-awakened perspective.

Expanding your consciousness helps you to avoid taking things personally. You're between a rock and a hard place because if you do as they wish, you give up your zone to BE in, and if you don't do as they please, you feel poorly for not obliging them. On the flip side, if you, as an awakened person, request something of someone and they say no to you, you don't need to lessen yourself by becoming indignant, hostile, or insulted for being turned down.

The sadness is that as a human being, all you want is to be accepted, wanted, and loved, but in this 3D consciousness, it comes with a high price because it means you must follow the rules or else. And no one wants to say it out loud, but we all know that feeling of a grueling empty pit in the stomach when someone takes love off the table. We each want the people closest to us to think kindly of us and not feel them pull away in disapproval. That is a part of your humanity, which is why it is so much easier to stay asleep in the role expected of you by not rocking the boat.

---

not feel the need to accommodate by reading between silent lines of expectation unless you choose to do this for your own reasons. The mastery is to BE and LOVE WHO YOU ARE, knowing it is enough. (Love is Enough, Be You),89

Exploring Your Humanity

We have all put love on the table and then taken it off again, learning to play the love game to survive and see that our needs are met. You might be subject to the cold tone on the other end of a phone call for not calling a person as often as they prefer, or an email signed less affectionately to show the same is an example.

It is understood why anyone would wish to stay in a state of slumber because it is safer not to ruffle feathers. And you can be a hypocrite with ease for that purpose by simply saying what the other person wants to hear rather than speaking your truth. In an awakened state, you've no reason to placate another if you have not bestowed the same esteem upon yourself first.

It's most amazing how we've been on both sides of experiencing conditional love, compared to unconditional love, which seems to only exist in the eyes of Mother-Father-God. If you've not collected the full glory within, you'll cower when someone rescinds their love, leaving you grasping for security; however, if indeed within your full steam, you will be less likely to be affected by someone's displeasure as they pull away. You may feel the sting but will not be governed by its harsh punishment, nor will it be enough to motivate behavior changes or dynamics outside of your regular disciplined practice to stay attuned to yourself.

You must take confidence in being awakened. Otherwise, the grief you can feel from not playing by the rules makes you wish you weren't so rebellious and maybe even start hating yourself for it. After all, at that moment, you cannot see that the hurt and rejection others might be reacting to is simply because they don't understand and especially don't understand themselves, not because you had a goal to harm them.

To make matters much worse, they will also be highly insulted if you get caught telling them a little white story to protect your privacy and whereabouts. They become indignant, asking why you couldn't tell them the truth and that there is no excuse to lie, failing to be

Journey to Awakened Consciousness

aware that they put you in a position to create a story because they don't accept anything other than what they believe is acceptable. Of course, that will be considered an outright lie which is inexcusable and never to be forgiven.

You cannot say the knife you feel in your heart is the same whether you tell the truth or don't tell the truth because it is a foreign concept to the unawakened, and it will not register. Telling a story or telling the truth still creates a gap of incredible aloneness; either way, no one seems to understand. You know, deep down, the other person feels wounded but cannot find a way to fill that void because they remain oblivious to their own true nature. That is what hurts.

A question to balance it all might be…Do you remain asleep until you get sick from so much imprisonment, or do you awaken and give every cell in your body freedom? The caveat is, either way, there is a price, except with the latter choice, at least you contain and enjoy a sense of personal freedom and peace in body, mind, and spirit for doing right by yourself. Someone might come close to understanding if they had travailed the path of an awakened journey and had learned to honor and respect themselves. Maybe then, they might come close to knowing how you feel.

Everyone comes from their school of beliefs, which may differ from your own, so even sharing with an awakened being will not necessarily guarantee a feeling of closeness. True intimacy must be entirely self-contained in marriage to self, or the temporary warm fuzzy feeling is fleeting. Feeling loved on a deep level is possible when you know without question that you are part of the Universe and can acknowledge I am one with all and all with the one. This encompassing expansion allows the comfort of knowing I am never alone.

Funeral for a Friend
Old Self Memorialized

    To properly christen the new self, the old self must be eulogized. One good way to do this is to prepare a service like you oversaw organizing a funeral for a best friend. You can imagine the setting, place, flowers, and music, all orchestrated by you.

    You are the main speaker for the event, so you will carefully go over everything you want to say about your friend (old self). In terms of the service being for you, you've probably already endured and heard enough self-criticism, so be sure to emphasize all the good things you want to remember. It is a way to preserve her memory, so she won't think you are eradicating her. It is in the honoring she will feel pacified and more likely to take her place in retirement, with any luck at all, resting eternally.

    For example, if she constantly bent over backward for others, you might exemplify her outstanding ability to care for family and friends. If she was set in her ways to the point of being stubborn, you could mention she had superb mental strength and tenacity. If the person used verbiage engaging in slang occasionally, you could praise them for being so colorful. If they had a temper and could become hostile if easily riled, they had a great passion for life. If there were tendencies toward living like a hermit, you could add the person loved to spend time with animals in nature. If they appeared sullen for no apparent reason, the person was empathetic and tuned into vibrations and energies that wouldn't register with most people.

    Suppose they were someone who could quickly become paranoid. In that case, there had been many past lifetimes where

Journey to Awakened Consciousness

persons that had been closest, friends and family members, turned on them without warning or notice, so they felt overly concerned about the quality of all relationships. If the person could impulsively jump into situations without thought or practicality at times, they had a great zest for new adventures in life. You get my drift.

Make sure every trait is acknowledged, and then bring the eulogy to a close with a song that might reflect the overall manner and attitude of the individual. You could include a candle lighting ceremony and put one candle on the altar for all the person's good points and another for all the not-so-good issues. Add a candlelight for all the people the person encountered within their lifetime, and each one is blessed with healing. Finally, you envision your love and appreciation for your friend's life and God's unconditional love as one flame burning brightly.

In closing, you may read specific names of persons or places you feel need to be mentioned to express gratitude for their participation in your friend's pathway. As you bow your head in silence, quietly honoring all the ways you were helped to wholeness by your old self and recall all the things about it that helped you Awaken.

So be it, and so it is.

A New Self Emerged
What if the Old Self Resurfaces?

After self-examination and re-posturing for alignment in new ways, including the complete understanding of the old ways, the old self will occasionally pop her head out of the coffin. Her reappearance can feel daunting when you sense her carrying on in a tirade about how she wasn't that bad and continues to market herself in your new life.

Being in a union with self has advantages, yet falling out of the marriage can feel grim. You start walking in your new self, and suddenly, the old one bursts out of the grave. I mean, you go to great lengths to bury the old self, even give a respectful eulogy and funeral service, and then bam, it only takes the shred of an old aspect to breathe life into her dead limbs.

It helps to have humor because it can feel terrible after expanding body-mind-spirit to represent union with God-self and then, within seconds, feel an old way being activated. If not checked immediately, it's off and running back into a herstory-history groove. When I see myself possibly relapsing, I remember I left a DNR stipulation...*do not relive it*. There within is the humor. You can compare your old self to an ex-partner. You may think fondly of the person and can send good thoughts their way, but you wouldn't ever want to get back together with them.

After all the hard work and sending the old self on vacation permanently, or whichever way you address her retirement, it can feel alarming that she steps back in at any time rather than allowing the new you to be fully in charge. Pretty brazen that she could forget her funeral and honoring ceremony. It is so overwhelming but

Journey to Awakened Consciousness

bound to happen as I reminded myself no one goes up to bat and bats a thousand, as the expression goes.

Humbly, learning to allow for the process and realizing that nothing is set in stone but more like a dance. Matters not if you are dancing with another person or yourself; the same consideration and kindness must apply to achieve lasting results. Acceptance is more helpful in promoting union than creating further separation by pushing her away as a solution. Anytime you want to bury the past, memory is sure to surface, so best to know that even though you've put your old self out of commission, her memory is always with you and a part of you, so less of a shock when the remnants flood.

Perhaps, the only inspiration is to deal with her, or it will be another round of reincarnation. That is sure to soften the process rather than put yourself in sabotage by resorting to old ways and tactics or, worse yet, self-destructive behaviors. It is part of the personality that wants to arrive at a specific destination and is adamant about never looking back. She just wants to get there and doesn't want to be wavering back and forth or face intense vulnerability daily.

Most of us want to feel confident and strong, but that has been unrealistic as the journey has gone for me. There have been many days of great uncertainty where I thought I knew something but realized I knew nothing. Many days aware my ways were sketchy, especially the ones I was sure of. Many days, the thought of love was just too risky, so best to go undercover with a bag of cookies. You ask for divine guidance and then rebuke it if it is too scary. You ask for someone to love and then start a list of why that person is unsuitable. On and on in your humanity, it goes. All you wish for, after all, is some sense of security.

Another planet very similar to earth will be here for those who wish to continue, but the only thought strong enough to keep me moving forward is that I am ascending and will not incarnate back

Exploring Your Humanity

here again. It's the motivation for not falling into the despair of failure or giving up syndrome, which gravitates to the old self because that is safe and familiar. Still, the old self certainly isn't supplying that for you, and it's not much of a safety net with your unfamiliar new self, so take solace in the fact that you know you are not choosing to be earthbound for another round of reincarnation.

For a short time anyway, until new self-whispers in your ear and you become aware that you cannot forget the new self-emerging, you should do your best to go with the flow. This process can feel so up and down you need clarification. It seems like you've got to be better, brighter, more aware, know better, and never let a now moment allude you, which is easier said than done when you feel like you're sinking in a pond of mud, but expected to see a shiny new now moment. To bounce back, it helps to quiet your thinker by letting go of any right or wrong and good or bad thinking. Remember, all these aspects simply seek shelter and wholeness, making it possible for the old self to merge with God-self.

To know they (aspects of self) don't mean to act out or escape things that are your highest joy requires much diligence in accepting each one for who and what they are and loving them unconditionally. In love, they recede and take a step back, for there is the awareness they are accepted and loved for what they are, so there is no need to continue playing out to gain rank. Ultimately, you trust that an appointed guide, guardian, or angel will assist if you make a massive mistake regarding your highest good and joy.

Knowing that intervention is possible will see you on to victory. It can feel the darkest just before the dawning light of new consciousness streaming through. The anxiety produced from this reality was calmed by my guide telling me if you are climbing up the mountain and fall near the summit, but get up, brush yourself off, and continue to the top, does anyone remember that you fell or simply that you got to the top! When I think of the number of failed

Journey to Awakened Consciousness

moments to BE, it is shocking how many times I could not capture the moment.

You can rehearse repeatedly, but it won't matter because all the rehearsal time in the world can never prepare you for a fresh new now moment delivered by the *free-from-time* universal. You can project, organize, and base life on theory or assumption, but creation doesn't come about by planning in thought. Instead, it is an activation of cellular molecules in the present formation based on contributing energies or lack of it.

Attempting to think a creation into existence requires much effort compared to utilizing the natural flow of energy shifts available. This translates to the new self's greatest challenge: Feeling the face of 3D consciousness where participation had previously shown no mercy by declining opportunities for the highest joy due to fear, now recognized in a split second when a similar choice resurfaces to claim.

Rigid thinking in terms of decision-making has only left the world stricken with toxins. When mistakes of the past start haunting you, rather than taking a loss, remember to talk to yourself gently by reaffirming that you are widening your perceptions for making the best possible choices that match self-love and self-care modalities. A note to self should include that you are expanding by not emphasizing right or wrong and good or bad decisions but focusing on learning instead. This keeps you and me expanding, growing, expanding into eternity.

Channeled Messages on Awakening

Channeled entries are often not received in a phrasing flow based on the standard English vocabulary rules.

Decree for Awakened Consciousness

I GIVE YOU a new decree: Conditions such as sickness, illness, and depression do not touch me, for I no longer recognize them, so they no longer gravitate toward me. I've disabled pop-ups, and now I am alerted to disabling consciousness that allures anything minimizing to me. I disqualify infringements of non-freedom and return any previous injuries, scars, wrinkles, emotional traumas, etc., to the consciousness and belief systems that created each irregularity. I honor it all since it was once a part of me, and as I weave each thread, old to new, first heartbeat to now heartbeat…upon my tapestry, freedom reigns supreme. I am the representation of Mother-Father-God-Goddess I AM. I reflect the consciousness of
holy and wholeness in the above, as *body, mind, and spiritual* union in the below. I am a breath full of the perfect imaging light that created me to be. I am divinely free. And so, the story goes.

Jesus

From: *The Voice of Ascension.*

Mental Ills and Wills
Hope for our Mad Society

Modern-day houses the capacity to transform currents of energy like an electrical conduit. Only in the case of thought-forms running amuck there's little chance of acutely shifting the vibrations. Only a few may know something outside the *'what you see is what you get'* modality. A syndrome that has blanketed the human senses allowing them to remain dulled in depression, lethargy, and apathy.

As the saying goes, it takes a few good men, and few good men equal, awakened beings who know that more is going on than meets the eye and are willing to speak up or act if needed rather than turn a blind eye. It's a date and time when you all are required to awaken to the realm of possibility that exists, and sadly, one where many human beings sit vacant, lacking self-love, therefore, quickly filled with various frequencies meant to keep mankind down and out to maintain control over them.

The old motto that says, if you cannot see it, it doesn't exist, falls below the standard of care needed if society is to be molded into a new timeframe and network. Applying what you already have using intuition and self-knowing is the heightened intelligence required for meeting the current demands of what societies have created in their youth. It is a common sense transformed into a sixth sense. The five senses are already overloaded, so the sixth sense is now called upon to detect and rectify what has formally gone unnoticed.

TV shows and movies have portrayed the sixth sense as an item of obscurity. All have been judged and reviewed on face-value findings, and there have been no criteria other than to make determinations on handling human beings based on their actions. This is where a sixth sense may be the most helpful because there are many people who, under controversial circumstances, slide by unnoticed because they've learned to nod, make the statements people expect to hear and display the appropriate behavior and speech to remain in all the good graces society would expect of you. You have often heard someone say that the person accused of wrongdoing was lovely, quiet, and caring. They won't ever understand how that person could be capable of committing a violent crime toward another person. And then you have the person who just couldn't hold any of it and left replies and even physical notes saying they wished to harm, hurt, and create chaos. In that case, someone was made aware, but too late before anything was done about it, even when proof existed.

Proof or no proof, everyone's training in the third dimension is book oriented on the methods and ideologies proven to work or simply set as a law because others have deemed that is the way to proceed. Now, with all the new currents, devices, and modes of operation, all are left just shaking their heads on finding any outside source to blame to feel better about what has run riot and out of control.

Human beings have always felt better when they have someone to blame because it alleviates them from having to dig deeper or invest themselves further for significant meaning and content as to why a situation exists in the first place. The blame handles all that by focusing on who did this or that, but what's left is the original problem. The original sin is never really addressed because what ensues is a battle over whose fault it is. All energies, therefore, are either to aggrandize the innocence of the innocent or continue to place blame and denigrate the accused, whether that be another individual or tenant others are living by.

Healing begins when someone stands up and announces that we've all been wrong. This is a place where all insinuations are neutralized in the vulnerability of not knowing what's the right or wrong thing to do, then a new day presents, and in neutrality, silent peace waves out like a river to all human beings in an unspoken flow of comradery and willingness to just be and coexist.

This is the grand unifier and hopes each of you craves at present. The reel coming together for the support and best interest of all. Let nothing get in the way of what you know or block your way if you don't.

Stay open solely and soulfully. Commander
J'nair DiBirk

Regarding Wasting Time
Silencing the Ticker

To accuse yourself of wasting time is to stay etched in the old paradigm tradition of clock-watching. Next to no movement at all because you've got the belief that you are not worthy, not participating in anything, thus, wasting time, which is a fallacy because you discount all the time you are simply being and breathing. It is poignant to merely sit and breathe, so there is no need to ignore your being.

You've got some harsh parameters on yourself and time to let go of some of these falsehoods taught by a generation that only understood doing, doing, and more doing. You barely rested even when ill. No time to sit idle for any reason was the philosophy of times past. In the present, though, of idle time lies ascension time, which places the sovereignty on the breath in and breath out as complete and whole.

Down to science, your scholars have defined everything by the amount of time it takes and then promote those who've found a shortened version or make the learning course easy as 1, 2, 3. Again, relating success as gauged according to time. No one gives you a medal or an award for expertly sitting and doing nothing because there is nothing to show for it in the physical realm.

The non-physical awards would be hard to classify because sitting would be unique for each person. One may incorporate bi-location or astral travel in their none-doing-time. In contrast, someone else might use the same opportunity to quietly slip into meditation. Another example could be tuning into a sense of timelessness via the past, present moments, or future, as given through feelings and visions. Being still allows for everything and is non-restrictive, so I encourage you to try it. Nothing to lose, only to gain via selfhood, that is.

In this new perspective, being lazy can be an asset. The demand you make good use of time has yet to do anything to procure well-being. It only causes various forms of neurosis, insomnia, anxiety, and depression because it is pressure driven.

Feel the power of creating divine time to eat, sleep, play, and work. Allow nothing to block your sense of timing and knowing. That flow may vary from person to person but is sure to produce optimum conditions for living at your best, especially if you've previously lived under the pressure of feeling the need to produce tangible results.

Father Time

The Collection Basket
Sentiments about Money by a Reformed Preacher

You could call me a senator because the same force of political energy that runs governmental agencies on behalf of the public is similar to what compelled me to compartmentalize my work, so people could see I was in it for them. Had to do this for people to have a sense of security since society depends on the organization and the rules designed to keep all safe and sound.

It's what most understand, a simple decree such as, if you do this, you'll get that, or do that to keep what you've got, so it didn't matter whether this framework included a promise of gaining entrance through the pearly gates or getting through passport control, it was the same. Mostly, guided to compliment the fact that the human mind has been programmed to understand and perceive in a structured way. Anything too liberal regarding preaching could be considered heresy, so even that was delivered with restrictions so that it would be accepted.

Anything that has worth certainly must cost something, and so it was. Looking back at my tenure as Reverend, I fully realize this. I had to include the collection of monies; otherwise, the congregation would not have given esteem and value to it. The collection of cash gave people the confirmation that they were indeed receiving something valuable.

If you let them walk away freely, they don't consider that what's been given has any importance. They don't feel inspired or motivated to return if they think it's too easy. This a powerful premise that all of life is based on, which is why most of your best sellers reflect how to make a million and succeed in business or be independently wealthy. In other words, without money or prestige, you're nothing.

Conversely, some best-selling novels are fiction because they allow a person to revel in fantasy, which is what the deeper part of self longs for. As if the pressure of making money and all that it deems in societal life creates so much personal stress, the fantasy of fiction becomes an outlet to seek relief from the struggle. Fairy book tales and stories soothe the pressure pitch of what makes the world go around. Money does make the world go around and is used accordingly to spoon-feed some small tenant that would reflect God's light in each human being present. You ask them literally to pay to be reminded of their higher self and soul light by someone like me.

They pay money for a place to sit in a church that reminds them of the goodness inherent within them. Pay money to decode the years of brainwashing to that degree. Pay something to earn their rights to be holy. You've got to pay for it is the verdict that's prevailed over much time in the third dimension.

Excellent, as I review my time on Earth and understand the simplest of facts in all considered sacred here, my holiness, my divinity, always comes freely because I am a child of God. But free never enticed anyone to claim their freedom. They are convinced throughout all time that it must be fought for, as any good war tells of. It's just that in this now, the fight, the struggle, and the journey are only with the self. All conflicts will ensue and continue simply due to the unrest within each individual.

An apocalypse is now a rendition of what happens when earnestness is placed on the outside measures of a man rather than on the merits of fortitude within. Trident as it may sound, this is the truth I express now without a collection. I vocalize the strength of redemption is available for free...it only requires a look inside the mirror image of thee. Since what you see in the mirror isn't always an indication of what you'll get, it is encouraged for each person to look beyond the image and remove any masks that may cover the true self. The authentic representation of the soul is one without a need to assuage or appear in a certain way to anyone else to be accepted and ensure getting your needs met, or to appear politically correct to sell your wares, rather than just be you.

Risky business, just to be you, in a society that demands appearances are everything. Even illusions are overlooked when someone falls out of contention with their expected role and image by violating the terms and conditions. The focus has never been on who the authentic person is because you have all been groomed to be a certain way. This programming was instilled in you when you arrived on Earth. As you grow and develop each year, the contingencies deepen as the plot thickens about who and what you're meant to be.

No wonder a person feels lost when they suffer a blow, a death, a breakup, or an incurable illness. None of the societal organizations has taught or prepared them to be with themselves, so there are no tools to fall back on when needed. Lost, because all assurances have been placed on what there is to gain if you are a proper member of your clan/village/city/country/etc. They don't groom you for how to handle situations when what you've got has been taken away or who to look to for answers. More searching on the outside, when the searching needs to be on the inside so you can find out what you truly need rather than let others decide that for you.

And it is free! Sadly, there has been no encouragement for this state of being, so I am coming forth now with a new pitch. Sadly, I was made painfully rich via these old ways. Still, it wouldn't have mattered because had I emphasized soul light and truth, it would have been considered hogwash to be poor but rich in spirit! To some degree, that's why Jesus himself, in a penniless preacher's words, was not valued by the governor of the time. Nothing to show. It must have touched a deep resonance within, or it wouldn't have played out to be a threat by the powers that ruled at the time. If recognized for what it was, it would have remained free.

Still, to this day, no one listens to a person with no money. They are considered less than, street people, orphans of the world that became wayward from lack of drive or lust for material riches. Easy enough to see why the mainstream still listens to money, property, and prestige. It's estimated that someone must've done something right if they got all that.

Conversely, if you've got nothing, you have nothing important to say or share because you've nothing to show. Interesting, though, how many spiritual preachers throughout time have not had much to speak of but continually reached out to the poor or to uplift those that failed according to these societal standards by not being able to acquire much.

Examples include Gandhi, Buddha, Jesus, the Dali Lamas', Francis of Assisi & Sister Clare. The pope and many other evangelist leaders gained great wealth. We knew to be valued, we must stand on a pedestal of wealth, fame, and fortune to be heard or respected. The one who walks barefoot in the street with only the cloak upon their shoulders is ostracized as a taboo figure with mental problems or just an inbred heretic looking to stir the pot. This is not meant to demoralize anyone, but in my current perspective, it all has merit.

How would anyone know another way had they not first adopted someone else's words and truth before their own? The learning continues, and each person's spiritual growth is unique. Let them all become valuable gems unto themselves. Do all you can to collect the real you, and onward, with all that is considered Reverend for you and me.

Billy Graham

Your Wings

The Sovereign State of Being encompasses the power to fly or walk gently on terra firm whenever you choose. The combination of strength and humility is a dynamic duo. Learning to fly can include many falls. Once mastered, you always remember what the expansion of self-awareness feels like. Modesty and compassion are the graces you share with anyone spreading their wings to practice flying. It always seems easier to judge yourself or others, but more of a stretch when you can show understanding by knowing firsthand the trials and tribulations of experimental flight.

The falls represent every time guilt or obligation turned up a rough landing. The dreadful feeling of letting yourself down, taking the fall, minimizing yourself repeatedly. Full take-off and successful landing are a victory of your authentic self being unencumbered. Stumble, you may, learning appropriate times and safety zones, but like everything else, human beings engage; practice does make perfect. Your bodies are invisible and movable. The mental, emotional, physical, and spiritual vehicles can be shifted upon request.

It is your birthright to leave the body and fly anywhere, and then to know the flight is a privilege and gift so that upon returning to the body, it is with gratitude. If you feel emotional pain, fly into a quiet cloud zone. If you need clarification on overthinking and analyzing, take flight by gliding over calm waters. If you are in physical discomfort, fly into a medical bed of immediate healing for reprieve and renewal from that suffering. Eventually, with much practice in shifting zones, the bodies will catch on to that quality and quickly relocate themselves into these places of peace and neutral territory instantaneously. Flight time reduced to zero. You are not abandoning yourself but instead locating peace in your *body, mind, and spirit* to dwell in the union of stillness. If an issue requires your attention, it presents much easier in calmness than getting stymied in the downtime of discomfort, which only hinders awareness.

The ability to fly also includes bilocating (to be in two places at once) should someone need immediate help. [13]* The miraculous ability to leave the body not only during nighttime when you sleep but also during daylight hours within seconds if need be. Both grounded and in-flight options come full circle in the remarkable phenomena of bilocation. Yes, it may feel like you are a prisoner in the human body and that your spirit remains confined there until you pass out of that physical shell. Yet, you are free anytime you choose to claim freedom. I share Wings of Freedom and Unlimitedness.

Archangel Raphael

---

[13] *Author's Note: I once had a vision of pushing someone out of the way from being hit by a car in the middle of a busy intersection in a crowded, highly populated city in Asia. Vivid and clear, however, no idea who the person was. I just know I was there.*

Union

On your list of things to do in everyday life, it would behoove you to add the most celebrated task of all: Shine a light onto tendencies, memories, or feelings that are not in sync with the fullness of who and what you are.

Suppose you understand the only thing that holds you back are these mere snippets of personality traits that look to reign supreme from a former time. In that case, you can domineer their threads of expression by decreeing them retired, out of duty, and no longer active.

The awareness that they may have gained momentum in a past existence will help prevent judging if they appear in your present embodiment. Embracing these aspects as a part of the whole will allow for a peaceful retirement. In contrast, rejection only promotes their constant recurrence as they struggle for your attention and acceptance.

Reflect the Golden Age, where all of you are not hampered by one of you. Awaken the many aspects that comprise your being, and in the awakening, vibrate to the golden light of your I AM essence. This re-emergence of self from the shadows of many lifetimes is your ticket for a smooth trip into the ascended state of being and onward dimensions.

Kuthumi

Smile Face

Strive for acceptance of the perfection that is you as is. It can be picture-perfect. One half of you may not match the other half. One ear may be larger than the other ear. You may have one arm longer than the other arm. If you gaze upon yourself in the mirror feeling distraught over your appearance or that you are not aesthetically pleasing, it becomes a sad face of dishonoring. I beckon: Honor every inch of you because it is heart light beaming through every cellular structure that broadcasts your true beauty like a lighthouse.

I encourage leaning into the achievement of physical self-acceptance. Avoid the urge to physically altar yourself, as this attempt to change what was masterminded by the God Force only creates disillusionment. A silkscreen at best. The emotional, mental, and spiritual bodies will follow suit once you acclaim physical acceptance as a perfect home temple for the light within that be you. In that vein, recognizing each body part in excellent condition and health simply because it is your soul light contained therewithin is mastery.

After all, dear ones, your heart light defines you as a child of God. It is your choice if you wish to masquerade the physical with a polished veneer, but that will only mirror a small percentage of your beingness. May you all attune to heart light and beam a smiley face confirming its registry accordingly. Yea, and so it shall be.

Dwal Khul

Gabriel's Halo

Beauty lies in the heart and soul of the beholder. Even though you live in a high fashion world where your experts of the day decide what is beautiful and fashionable, that expression remains for you to explore and display uniquely in your way. Once you choose that, you no longer need to fit in and experience more of a desire to simply be who and what you are. That is the halo over your head, my eyes see.

Archangel Gabriel

Steer Clear of the Curb

Sabotage comes in forms yet defined, and good to understand in terms of the detours, the excuses, and/or reasons to leave self at curbside. Nevertheless, God helps those who help themselves, and see God/Goddess, what flows in, to help you barricade off any threatening detour or side journeys opposing the highest good and joy. And so, it is.

Jeanne de Arc

Claim Peace

Be indebted to nothing. Incur no debt. Command and take credit for the fullness of your essence, even if you may regret certain words and actions. Know that any overflow or spill of your energy, good, bad, or indifferent, becomes an opportunity for another person to claim and understand the core of their being. A way to push for peace without the force of an army. Every day offers the chance to accrue more inner peace. When you realize peace is the only outcome that matters, words of expression are unnecessary. The peace you harbor within is enough.

Hanuman

In Your Own Time

Time is the oldest living agent. The dinosaur age has come and gone, yet in some respects, we've seen many examples of dinosaurs still roaming. The aggression transpired when this animal was pursuing its prey, food, or basic survival needs and is not much different from the motion of human beings stampeding in 3D. These energetic time sequences are still in motion to varying degrees. However, in this New Age of continual shifting, it would benefit all to feel the force of panic and fear, cease and desist.

How to know if you are operating in this archaic paradigm would be if you catch yourself pushing or rushing to seize a target. The hustle and bustle for food, money, property, goods, or possessions would be the notification. More in accord is the light flooding Earth and opening a new dimensional frequency to reside, where you simply fall into the distinctive light energy of each day. You may be thinking to yourself, invisible, therefore, unclaimable. The goal will manifest automatically when an appropriate proportion of light has been gathered and opened for its purpose. A fluid reward.

In short, if this principle is applied to daily living, life will flow easily, especially when life's extremes can cause fluctuations that produce confusion and congestion. Allow me to assist by requesting your energy release from the old stations of the cross pathways, knowing now there is no longer a need to follow the order of any previously marked passageway. Jump from point to point if you please, bypassing the diligent order of A thru Z. B and P may be all you need to visit in that grouping.

Create your operational hours; no need to retire if energy is still available at 10 pm. Like waking hours, if the momentum opens at 5 am, let that energy support you, rather than feel a need to plant yourself there until 8 am just because. It is necessary now to recognize your body's biorhythms and how those inclinations are responding to your mind and spirit. ¹⁴* And so it is. Let yourself lighten up and be at ease.

Sponsored by Yeshua and Ptolemy V

---

¹⁴ *Author's Note: My original due date to be born was November 19th, and instead, I made my earthly debut on September 19th, so I consider this one of the ways I was already operating out of order.*

The Overhead of God's Timing

This is a time in 3D of not knowing which end is up. The disoriented feeling of not knowing where you are, what day it is, who you are, or what you are doing signifies a merger of time and space. Momentary lapses of time and being out of the body are ways a person might cope with the renewal.

In such a pocket, when you find yourself looking around with a where am I pause, it is an opportunity to breathe in the way you are repositioning yourself in the Universe. The blending of experiences on your eternal timeline from beginning to present waves over and leaves you the feeling that something is missing, when in reality, what was forgotten just slips into the now moment giving you a sense of feeling lost since you are not used to carrying this memory with you daily.

Vulnerability flushes these spaces, for in the memory is contained other time spaces where an individual endured physical, mental, and emotional wounds, characterized by the intensity of seeming to be occurring in your present time frame. It can leave a person feeling very exposed and without shelter as they navigate in a blend of times previously inaccessible.

What appears in dreamtime, including visions of persons that seem menacing or creatures that look repulsive, are remnants of old stories wanting to be sure you didn't forget about them and helpful to remember they cannot hurt you in this now. It is this perspective that will set you free from worry, anxiety, and doubt. As awareness opens of all you've ever been, you may also collect bits of things important you've forgotten over time, which might feel refreshing. The dreary daily news can be uplifted when you are reminded of why you've come to Earth and the impact it will have on all human creation.

Your care has not gone unnoticed. Consider mapping all the spots on Earth you wish for love to touch upon and then see it land there, connect it with your heart and soul, and know it is done. No time to vacillate. This a great time to BE the light with complete assurance that everything you need is within you to master change in every place you care about by simply directing the attention of your love and care there. It doesn't seem like enough, yet it's within the practice where confidence ushers in a new sense of your mastery's fullness. In a breath, this concept feels like a gigantic step being certifiably yours. Champion of Human rights, master me.

Master Yi

Epilogue - Ascension Note

Ascended, what it *does not* mean:

- Committed suicide.
- Passed from a terminal illness or lay the physical body down in the condition we call death.
- Called it quits by disappearing into the hills someplace to starve.
- Got depressed, drank too much alcohol, or took too many pills.
- Departed earthly life, heartbroken.
- Attributed the word success to acquiring things such as homes, cars, children, animals, possessions, and/or worldly goods.

What Ascension *does* mean:

- Return home to Mother-Father-God in wholeness.
- Unconditional love
- No cruelty to another person, animal, planet, place, or thing
- Took the best possible care of my physical body. I also honored my mental and spiritual bodies, bringing home all aspects, including current personality traits, along with any lifetime energies that represented fear or discord while in human form, achieving unity in mind, body, and spirit whenever possible.

- Walked out my time on Earth, even though I've been feeling complete here for some time. Waited for the divine moment when Mother-Father- God/Goddess and my Master Guide Ascended Master Saint Germain and cosmic father, Ashtar, notify me of the opportunity to Ascend.
- I was awakened to the realization that some of my dreams were shattered, but I could still hold each of them in love and peace and be pleased that someone else, someplace on this planet, is living these same dreams in joy.
- No further need to reincarnate.
- All lessons learned, agreements kept, with all the love in my heart for everyone in my life/lives, when invited to step aboard the spacecraft, I answered with a "Yes, I Am ready to ascend, having completed my primary mission for Earth's ascension process, I am choosing to be reunited and back home with my cosmic family."
- Will not be able to locate or find a body identified as Paula Bourassa. As a *lightbody,* it will be lifted off Earth and transform itself into pure light essence.
- Balanced the use of my God-Given free will, never to stray again from the unconditional love of my soul, honoring self, and respecting every other form of life, every living thing, here, there, and everywhere.

I know this is hard to understand. Ascension [15]* is the wave of your future. This communication is not meant to solicit grief, melancholy, anger, fear, drama, or trauma. It is intended to celebrate

---

[15] *Author's Note:* Any living thing or form can choose Ascension, including humans, animals, birds, planets, stars, galaxies, and solar systems.

that one human being was complete with her earthly walks and didn't have to experience a physical death to exit the third dimension.

Many of you know you are here to be part of Ascension and have retained some remembrance. Some will think it is a strange concept only portrayed in the movies. Doesn't matter. Planet Earth will ascend no matter what. She is next in line.

This will happen, despite every ditch effort to hold her as a possession by those brothers and sisters who are not pro-ascension. I am not judging these beings, only acknowledging they have not fully claimed their own I AM essence, so they will continue making egocentric choices, motivated only by the need to keep control and possess things.

I have given my example of Ascension so that when the time comes and a choice is offered to ascend, you will not hesitate if you feel complete in human form and step onto the craft sent for you. To beam up and onward into future existence based on your soul's highest choice.

Also, remember what I've described is my current understanding of how I will Ascend. Suppose that has shifted compared to the version written here. In that case, it may occur slightly differently as evolution and involution are in constant flux, so allowances will always be made for last-minute changes. Nothing is black and white, there are probably an *unlimited number of ways* to Ascend, and these may be shown to you as they are conceived and developed.

My highest version of Ascension is to be collected and welcomed aboard Ashtar's flying craft. He is known to some of you as The Commander, and I am proud to be a member of his family. Ashtar is like a bouncer at a nightclub. Only his job entails watching over all of Earth and bouncing out influences or beings utilizing fear-based tactics to interfere with the Ascension Process, or in plain terms, not behaving well.

Some proof of this may be left behind to give you confidence. Earth will ascend no matter what; that is a given. Your scientists have already found another planet with similar features as Planet Earth, although it will not be called Earth. It will be available for those of you who are not choosing to ascend and would like to continue in your earthly ways. Freewill choice will always be honored as it has always been.

I am grateful to have been with Gaia during her time at Ascension. Feeling blessed to have shared my love and appreciation for all the lifetimes she has allowed my feet to walk upon her breast and my body to be buried in her Earth...*she is a soul too*. Blessed Am I, I Am.

If you have claimed the sovereignty of love and respect for yourself, then it is only natural that you extend the same honor to every other person, animal, place, thing, or land on Planet Earth and onwards. In nature, there has been nothing but pure joy for me with all the walks, hikes, and lovely views. The only hurt and disappointment have been noticing someone's picnic trash strewn about the land and water. For this disrespectful act against the planet, I will continue to hold space for each of you to clean up your insides so that you can clean up your outsides. Beautify.

My passion is assisting Planet Earth and anyone else choosing to Ascend.

Bibliography

Bourassa, Paula, and Ascended Master Kuthumi. *Love is Enough.* LuLu.com, 2012 (Be You, Page 89)

Herbert Puryear, *The Edgar Cayce Primer.* Association of Research and Enlightenment, (A.R.E.) Virginia Beach, Virginia 1985

Bourassa, Paula. *Truth with No Proof.* Amazon 2017 (excerpts page 166)

Bourassa, Paula. *The Voice of Ascension.* Amazon 2018 (excerpt pages 16-20)

Judge, William Q. *Bhagavad-Gita.* Los Angeles: The Theosophy Company, 1986 (Excerpt pages 41)

Hurtak, J.J. (1977) The Book of Knowledge: *The Keys of Enoch.* Los Gatos: The Academy for Future Science www.keysofenoch.org (Excerpt 169, 191)

Hudson, Thomas Jay Ph.D. *The Law of Psychic Phenomena.* New York: Samuel Weiser, 1968 (excerpt 104, 184)

Norman, Ernest L. *Tempus Procedium.* El Cajon: Unarius Science Of Life, 1965 (excerpt page 105)

Also, written by Paula Bourassa

Love is Enough
(By Paula & Ascended Master Kuthumi)

One Defining Moment
(By Paula, Inspired by Lord Buddha)

Truth with No Proof

It's Never Quite What You Think
(By Grace)

The Voice of Ascension

Junie's Story

www.ingramcontent.com/pod-product-compliance
Lightning Source LLC
Chambersburg PA
CBHW070521030426
42337CB00016B/2045